Theories of Attraction
and Love

By

Donn Byrne, Professor of Psychology, Purdue University

George C. Homans, Chairman, Department of Sociology, Harvard
    University

John Lamberth, Assistant Professor of Psychology, University of
    Oklahoma

Bernard I. Murstein, Professor of Psychology, Connecticut College

Theodore M. Newcomb, Professor of Psychology & Sociology,
    University of Michigan

Elaine B. Walster, Professor of Psychology & Sociology, University
    of Wisconsin

Robert F. Winch, Professor of Sociology, Northwestern University

Theories of
Attraction
and
Love

Editor

Bernard I. Murstein

S P

Springer Publishing Company, Inc., New York

Copyright © 1971

SPRINGER PUBLISHING COMPANY, INC.
200 Park Avenue South, New York, N. Y. 10003

Library of Congress Catalog Card Number: 77-172067
Standard Book Number: 0-8261-1290-0

Printed in U.S.A.

Designed by Vicki Kessinger

To Otello Desiderato,
the noblest Buiese of them all

Preface

There can scarcely be any question that interest in the area of interpersonal attraction has accelerated sharply in recent years. Perhaps it is because, in a country which for a number of years has seemed to be poised on the brink of disaster and woefully unable to achieve internal harmony within its borders, the ability to relate meaningfully to one's fellow-man seems as elusive as the Holy Grail. Perhaps it is no more than the inevitable consequence of man's continually emerging sense of individuality. Man is more free than before, but the security gained from tradition, habit, and living in a given community all of one's life has been left behind with the past. To relate meaningfully to one's fellow-man is scarcely as easy in this transient world as it was one hundred years ago. When economic circumstances provide sufficient leisure, man seeks to find a more meaningful rationale than material wealth for his existence. Clearly, his search centers on the quality and quantity of his interpersonal relationships.

The price of this late awakening, however, is that our knowledge of why two people are drawn to each other is still relatively incomplete. We do not lack for theories, but many of these theories are elementaristic and badly in need of emendation. It was for this purpose, therefore, that the Symposium at which these papers were given was organized. The participants were chosen because they represented a wide variety of theoretical backgrounds. Since it was deemed necessary to avoid the narrowness sometimes found in wholly psychological or sociological theories, both sociologists and psychologists were represented among the contributors. For the most part, the psychologists who participated were thoroughly conversant with major sociological viewpoints, as were the sociologists with respect to psychological thinking. The task of each of the five speakers, Donn Byrne, George C. Homans, Bernard I. Murstein, Theodore M. Newcomb, and Elaine Walster, was to prepare a paper which represented his latest theoretical thinking on interpersonal attraction in the dyad. Robert F. Winch very kindly consented to serve as the discussant of the five papers. (John Lamberth, co-author with Donn Byrne, was not present at the meeting.)

The Connecticut College Symposium on Theories of Interpersonal Attraction in the Dyad convened for two days (October 15, 16, 1970) on the College campus. The moderator for the first day's session, at which Professors Newcomb, Byrne, and Homans presented their papers, was Professor Otello Desiderato. On the second day, Professor Eleanore B. Luckey served as the moderator for the papers of Professors Walster, Murstein, and Winch. Discussion followed the presentation of each paper, and each author was offered the opportunity to revise his paper for presentation in this volume in the light of the discussions and to add any commentary that he wished.

To serve as an introduction and summary of some of the theorectical viewpoints utilized by the various authors, I added an additional chapter. This was deemed necessary because the authors were presenting their latest thinking and not striving to outline a theory with which their name had been linked. It is hoped that this first chapter will serve as a guide to individuals relatively unacquainted with the major theories of interpersonal attraction and encourage them to pursue these topics more thoroughly in some of the sources listed in the references for each chapter. The book itself is addressed to both students and scholars in the disciplines of sociology, personality, and social psychology.

June, 1971   *Bernard I. Murstein*
New London, Connecticut

Acknowledgments

Many persons served as midwives to the birth of the Symposium. My thanks are due first to the contributors to this volume whose vigorous participation in the Symposium not only provided the warp and woof of this book but served also as a vigorous catalyst for intellectual stimulation for students, faculty, and townspeople who attended the sessions. Thanks are due also to Eleanore B. Luckey and Otello Desiderato who served as moderators of the sessions and to Betty Morrison, Helen F. Dayton, Eleanore H. Voorhees and the students and staff who gave nobly of their time and effort to provide the material comforts of life to the participants at the Symposium. Margaret L. Thomson, director of the News Office, helped to bring the symposium to the attention of the public. June C. Hughes and Fay Bomberg did much of the typing of the manuscript.

President Charles Shain of Connecticut College, in a year when the College was under severe financial pressure, nevertheless saw fit to grant the funds which made this endeavor possible and further earned my gratitude by graciously welcoming the participants and opening the Symposium. John H. Detmold and Charles A. Edwards of the College Development Office tirelessly searched for possible sources of financial support. I am therefore indebted both to them and to the Shell Companies Foundation and the National Science Foundation who provided the financial support that made the Symposium possible.

I wish to thank the following publishers and authors for permission to use quotations from their books and periodicals: Academic Press, Inc.; American Psychological Association; Basic Books, Inc., Publishers; Chandler Publishing Company; Dell Publishing Company, Inc.; Hogarth Press Ltd.; Holt, Rinehart & Winston, Inc.; Houghton Mifflin Company;

Alfred A. Knopf, Inc.; Little, Brown and Company; David McKay Company, Inc.; Meredith Corporation; National Council on Family Relations; University of Nebraska Press; Oxford University Press; The Philosophy of Science Association; Plenum Publishing Corporation; John Wiley & Sons, Inc.; and Robert F. Winch. Full citation is given in the chapter in which the copyrighted material appears.

B. I. M.

Contents

1

Critique of
Models of Dyadic Attraction

Bernard I. Murstein

The symposium at which the papers in this book were first presented and discussed dealt with theories of love and attraction in the dyad. Each of the participants presented some of his most recent thoughts on the topic of attraction or love rather than giving an elementary exposition or review of the basic theoretical underpinning which launched this latest work.

It may be helpful to the reader who is relatively unfamiliar with the literature on interpersonal attraction, therefore, to have some basic approaches to the study of attraction ("learning," "exchange," and "balance") briefly described and evaluated.* The specific commentary on the five speakers' presentations falls to the province of the discussant, Professor Winch (see Chapter 7).

BEHAVIORAL REINFORCEMENT

Although among the lower phyla attraction often appears to be influenced by instinct and imprinting, many attraction theorists adhere to

* For reading and commenting on this chapter I am indebted to Donn Byrne, Otello Desiderato, Arthur C. Ferrari, George C. Homans, Theodore M. Newcomb, Regina Roth, Robert F. Winch, and J. Alan Winter. Despite this formidable array of readers, there are doubtless errors of commission and of omission, and these, needless to say, are mine.

1

some kind of reinforcement model in studying interpersonal attraction. Attraction might be conceptualized as "a positive linear function of positive reinforcements received from [another]" (Byrne & Nelson, 1965, p. 662), or, as Homans views it, "In choosing between alternate courses of action, an individual chooses the one for which the perceived value of the result multiplied by the perceived chances of obtaining it is the greater."*

But, if every action an individual makes is by definition the most rewarding (reinforcing) under the circumstances, the number of possible rewards must be legion. Rewards may be readily discernible when they come in the form of material wealth, praise, and demonstrations of competency. Suppose, however, a man buys his girl friend furs and a bullwhip so that she may don the furs and whip him soundly to his cries of masochistic ecstasy. Is the behavior of this *Venus in Furs* rewarding to him? The answer should still be yes, because taste and pleasure are, after all, individual things.

Suppose, however, that a woman marries a man who, it later develops, is a victim of "demon rum." Let us further suppose that he is unable to hold a job, that he is insulting, and that he beats his wife and children. Why does she stay with him? Perhaps she is Catholic and believes that divorce would be a greater sin than that which he commits against her daily. Her adherence to her Catholicism rewards her more than the beatings she receives disconcert her. Perhaps he has a lot of money, and she believes that his liver will succumb before she does, making her a wealthy heiress. Or perhaps she has stared wistfully at the mirror, recoiled from the apparition she saw there, and accurately forecast that she could hardly expect to do much better elsewhere. Staying with her husband, therefore, is only rewarding in the sense that it is less aversive than the ills which might beset her if she left him.

Because so many behaviors can be reinforcing either by being highly satisfying or merely less aversive than strongly aversive behaviors, the question arises as to how reinforcing behavior can be distinguished from nonreinforcing behavior? According to a Skinnerian learning model, response probability is one way of determining whether reinforcement has taken place. If the probability of a response which has been followed by a stimulus is increased, we may conclude that this stimulus is reinforcing for the respondent.

Unfortunately, in real life, and even in controlled laboratory experiments, it is often difficult to determine *why* a stimulus may be rein-

* Personal communication by George C. Homans.

forcing. A case in point is provided by an experiment of Golightly and Byrne (1964). These authors hypothesized that similar and dissimilar attitudes could serve as positive and negative reinforcers in a learning situation. They conducted a simple discrimination learning task in which similar and dissimilar attitude statements served as reinforcements. The task involved a card containing a circle and square; one of the figures was black, the other white; one was large and the other small. All possible combinations of size, shape, color, and position were randomly presented, but the discrimination to be learned was small-large; small was correct for half of the subjects, large for the other half.

After each correct response, an attitude statement similar to the subjects' own beliefs was presented, and after each incorrect response a dissimilar statement was presented. The effect was to change response probability in favor of choosing the large-small dimension.

Two other groups of subjects also were employed. One of these was a traditional reward-punishment group for which the selection of the desired response was followed by a card saying "RIGHT," with the wrong selection eliciting a card saying "WRONG." Not surprisingly, this group proved even more effective than the attitude-group in changing their response probability. Last, a control group received neutral attitude statements, and this group showed essentially no change in response probability.

Golightly and Byrne concluded that their hypothesis that similar and dissimilar attitude statements could serve as positive and negative reinforcers was confirmed, since the attitude group was significantly superior to the control group both on overall performance and linear trend.

It is possible to argue, however, that the subject merely noted the fact that similar attitude statements tended to follow a specific kind of stimulus dimension (e.g., largeness), whereas dissimilar items followed a variety of possible stimulus dimensions (color, shape, position) which, therefore, would be much more difficult to conceptualize as belonging to any class of attitude statements. In other words, it is possible that there was nothing intrinsically rewarding about similar attitude statements in a setting which ostensibly had nothing to do with attitudes. The effectiveness of the similar statements thus may have depended only on their serving as cues to what the subjects took to be the correct response. To be sure, the experimenter did not say that the largeness-smallness dimension was the "correct" answer in this group, but the fact that it was the only learning discrimination paired with one class of attitude statement may have suggested its correctness. The reinforcement may have been, therefore, the feeling of competency in having solved the task by noting a relationship between a stimulus dimension (largeness-smallness) and a class of attitude statements (similar).

The problem of whether similar statements were intrinsically rewarding or merely served as cues to the correct response could have been resolved through the use of another group. This group could choose between the largeness-smallness dimension followed by a dissimilar statement and any other dimension followed by a similar statement. If the probability of choosing the largeness-smallness dimension increased after a block of trials as before, the cue explanation would be the valid one. If subjects now chose any dimension except the largeness-smallness one, the Golightly and Byrne conclusions would be more strongly supported than before.

The problem of determining why something is reinforcing is infinitely more complicated once one leaves the delimited laboratory experiment. Consider the mythical Connecticut Congressman, Phineas Fogbottom, who, learning that one of his constituents has been laid off by an aeronautics concern, is instrumental in directing him to another company. Suppose he helps several people in this way. We may assume that helping these individuals is rewarding, but what about it is rewarding? Is it Fogbottom's love of mankind that promotes this behavior, his self-image as a kindly person, his idea that he is creating gratitude which will gain him future votes, or his concern about the business interests in his state? Perhaps each of them plays a part in varying degree. It appears clear, in any event, that it would be most difficult if not impossible to determine which of these reasons rewards his behavior. Response probability, in sum, can tell us that *something* is rewarding, but in complex cases it cannot tell us what there is about the rewarding behavior that makes it rewarding. By further research, each of the aforementioned reasons for aiding the worker could be tested. Will the Congressman, for example, help an unemployed Rhode Island worker even if his deed receives no notice in Connecticut? He should do so if his aid is not dictated by political motives. However, for practical reasons, it is unlikely that experimental controls could be applied to this problem.

Are we making too much of this lack of knowledge of *why* certain responses are rewarding? After all, isn't it enough to be able to determine that a response is rewarding even if we can't be sure we know why it is rewarding? Unfortunately, in the study of human behavior the *why* is very important. Consider the heiress whose charms are praised by a suitor. So long as she believes that the suitor cares for her, the heiress finds his words perfume to her ears. If she concludes that the motivation for his hitherto delightfully rewarding words are based on his love of her money rather than of herself, the very same words become anathema. Attraction for human beings, therefore, is heavily influenced by implied motives as well as behavior.

Keeping the strengths and weaknesses of reinforcement theory in mind, let us examine two somewhat different reinforcement models, "learning" and "exchange," and see how adequately they treat attraction.

A Learning Model of Interpersonal Attraction

The greatest amount of research in adapting a learning model to the study of interpersonal attraction has been undertaken by Byrne and his associates, although the Lotts (Lott & Lott, 1965) also have contributed greatly to the literature. Attraction is defined by Byrne and Clore (1970) as being "one of a more general class of evaluative responses." Using a classical conditioning model, a variety of stimuli such as similarity of attitudes, for example, are assumed to function as unconditioned stimuli. Similarity may be presumed to elicit a positive evaluative response in most individuals because they basically like and accept themselves. It should be noted, however, that similarity is but one of a number of reinforcers. For example, evaluation of the subject as "decent" or as a "rotter" and the status of the individual expressing the attitudes are two other possible reinforcers. It is true, nevertheless, that the vast majority of data stemming from Byrne's laboratory have focused on similarity.

The explanation of how Byrne's learning model would operate with respect to similarity is as follows: Let us call our subject, a normal, self-respecting individual, P. Another individual, O, may serve initially as a neutral stimulus. If O advocates attitudes and/or expresses personality characteristics which P perceives as similar to his own, O becomes associated with the pleasant feeling (reinforcement) which P experiences whenever his views are given consensual validation by another. The strength of the response is presumably determined by the traditional variables of classical conditioning: duration of the interstimulus interval, intensity of the stimulus, the reinforcing value of the stimulus to the individual.

The overt evaluative responses of a person are mediated by the conditioned covert affective responses and may be expressed by preferences for working with another, attraction towards him socially, or dislike. The overall attraction towards another is a function of the relative number of rewards and punishments associated with him (Byrne, 1969). The specific formula used by Byrne is found on page 63.

The paradigm most frequently utilized by Byrne has been that of the bogus stranger. A subject who has filled out an attitude questionnaire earlier is presented with the same questionnaire allegedly filled out by another subject. In reality, the protocol has been filled out by the experimenter so as to be dissimilar, partly similar, or highly similar to that of the real subject. On another questionnaire measuring liking for and willingness to work with the bogus stranger, the subject's attraction for him is predicted nicely by a simple linear gradient of the proportion of similar statements. There have been a wide number of variations on this central paradigm with personality items used as well as attitudes, and the stimulus characteristics of the bogus stranger varied (Negro, male, schizophrenic, child, socioeconomic status, physical attractiveness, etc.). In addition, Byrne and his associates have performed experiments in real life situations as well, of which more shortly.

There can be scarcely any question that Byrne has demonstrated the strong influence of similarity on attraction *within the confines of his paradigm*. The question arises as to how meaningful these findings are for behavior in more naturalistic settings. The ability to control all the variables except the one to be experimentally manipulated is a powerful tool in assessing the impact of variables such as similarity in a wide variety of situations. However, the proof of the pudding lies in the ability to utilize the knowledge gained thereby in more realistic situations, since the laboratory often cannot, and indeed is not intended to, mimic real life conditions.* Byrne himself has shown keen awareness of the limitations of laboratory research in his statement that

> ... if all an experimental subject knows about a stranger is that he holds opinions similar to his own on six out of six political issues, the stranger will be liked (Byrne, Bond & Diamond, 1969). We cannot, however, assume that any two interacting individuals who agree on these six issues will become fast friends because 1) they may never get around to discussing those six topics at all, and 2) even if these topics are discussed, six positive reinforcements may

---

* It should be stressed that no objection is made to the use of the experimental method in the study of interpersonal attraction. Objection is made only to the use of experiments which are so constructed as to inadequately represent the role of the variables in question in actual life.

simply become an insignificant portion of a host of other positive
and negative reinforcing elements in the interaction. A second
barrier to immediate applicability of a laboratory finding lies in the
nature of the response. It is good research strategy to limit the
dependent variable [in Byrne's data "liking" is the sum of two seven-
point rating scales], but nonlaboratory responses may be as varied
and uncontrolled as the stimuli. The relationship between that
paper-and-pencil measure of attraction and other interpersonal responses is only beginning to be explored (e.g., Byrne, Baskett, &
Hodges, 1969; Efran, 1969). The third barrier lies in the nature of
the relationship investigated. For a number of quite practical
reasons, the laboratory study of attraction is limited in its time span
and hence might legitimately be labeled the study of first impressions. Whether the determinants of first impressions are precisely the
same as the determinants of a prolonged friendship, of love, or of
marital happiness is an empirical question and one requiring a great
deal of research. (Byrne, Ervin, & Lamberth, 1970, p. 158).

Byrne, Ervin, and Lamberth (1970) found that in a "real life" situation, attitude-similarity on a questionnaire could predict attraction in a
30-minute "coke" date. A 30-minute "coke" date, however, is of itself
insufficient to allow much more than superficial observations of each other
by the couple, and more research is necessary on more lengthy and enduring relationships. Already, nevertheless, there are discrepancies between
Byrne's laboratory findings and "real life" findings that require clarification and explanation.

Byrne and his associates, for one thing, have found that attitude and
personality similarity strongly influence attraction (Byrne, 1969). In
studies of actual relationships among friends and spouses, on the other
hand, positive correlations between attitudes are frequently reported,
but correlations for personality characteristics typically have been either
low positive or of zero order (Day, 1961, Izard, 1960a, 1960b, 1963;
Fiedler, 1953; Miller, Campbell, Twedt & O'Connell 1966; Reader &
English, 1947; Backman & Secord, 1952; Reilly, Commins, & Stefic, 1960).

Another difference in findings concerns the role of the ideal-self in
attraction. Using the Byrne paradigm, Griffitt (1966) obtained self and
ideal-self measures for subjects. The bogus stranger's self-concept was
arranged so that it was of varying degree of similarity to the self and
ideal-self of the actual subjects. As usual, attraction was found to be a
function of similarity to the subject's self-concept, but neither a function
of similarity to the subject's ideal-self nor to self-ideal-self discrepancy.

These results are contrary to the findings of such researchers (among a multitude) as Thompson and Nishimura (1952), McKenna, Hofstaetter and O'Connor (1956), Beier, Rossi and Garfield (1961), Kipnis (1961), and Murstein (1971).

The first three studies cited above convincingly demonstrated that the best friends of the subjects tended to be perceived as closely approximating the subjects' ideal-selves. In her especially penetrating study, Kipnis was able to discover the dynamics behind these perceptions. Subjects whose best-liked roommates were perceived as possessing many more idealized qualities than the "self" tended to gain in the favorability of self-perception at a later date. Subjects whose best friends were not perceived as superior to the self tended to be more likely than the first group to drop the best friend. Apparently, we choose friends we idolize in the hope that some of their qualities will rub off on us.

Last, Murstein obtained self and ideal-self measures from couples who were engaged or seriously contemplating marriage. He correlated the self and ideal-self for each subject and then, using this correlation as a variable, obtained the correlation between members of the couples. He found a correlation of .43 ($p < .01$) over all couples and an even higher correlation of .56 ($p < .01$) for those couples who six months later were classified as having made good courtship progress. The couples, thus, chose a partner whose self-ideal-self correlation was approximately on a par with their own.

What are the reasons for the different findings between the Byrne et al and Griffitt's findings and all of the other studies? One difference lies in the different stages of relationship measured. The Byrne group focussed on initial impressions, whereas many of the other studies investigated ongoing relationships. But the fact that different stages of relationship were studied may offer more hope of reconciling the findings than really exists.

Although attitude similarity between friends or between spouses is generally found in most studies, it is not difficult to understand why personality similarity is such a weak, almost nonexistent finding. Attitude similarity may provide consensual validation that one is perceiving the world in accordance with an esteemed other, but it is not likely to influence the roles taken in a relationship between two people. Personality needs, however, do more readily translate themselves into roles. A dominant man might have trouble relating to his wife if she is also high on dominance. A dependent wife, on the other hand, would prefer to lean on a resourceful, nondependent husband.

Making the situation still more complicated is the fact that roles more than attitudes will vary with the specific context. The president of the

Lions Club may be a roaring monarch at the office but assume more lamb-like qualities when confronting his wife. To understand why personality similarity and attitude similarity inevitably are precursors to attraction in the Byrne and colleagues' studies while similarity to the ideal-self is not, we need to take a look at the paradigm employed by them.

We note first that in the typical personality similarity study (Byrne, Griffitt, & Stefaniak, 1967) as well as in the usual attitude paradigm (Griffitt, 1966), the subjects never interacted with the stranger, since the latter did not exist. The subjects therefore, could form no reaction to the physical appearance of the stranger, toward his dress, his religion, and the manner in which he greeted the subject. The *only* information the subjects possessed was the alleged protocol of the stranger. In short, there could only have been three possible reactions with regard to similarity. The subjects could have liked the stranger as a function of similarity, disliked him as a function of it, or been indifferent to the factor of similarity.

If the population consisted of neurotically disturbed persons who disliked themselves, there might have been a chance of a negative or zero order relationship between similarity and interpersonal attraction. Most college students, however, do not dislike themselves so much as to dislike anyone similar to themselves; consequently, the only probable alternative was that they would like the stranger who was similar to them.

But what of Griffitt's finding that the ideal-self score and the self-ideal-self discrepancy were not related to interpersonal attraction? Note that the subject has never interacted with the stranger. Probably, in his mind, he may never do so. Even if he does, it will be of a restricted, superficial nature as occurs in most experiments. What does it matter then whether this stranger professes one set of ideals or another or whether he is similar to the subject's ideal-self—surely an abstract piece of information for such a limited encounter. What is relevant is the stranger's attitudes and/or his personality. Given only one piece of information—that the stranger is or is not similar—it is hardly startling that only similarity to the self influences attraction.

It is necessary to ask what relevance this finding has for understanding human behavior? The Byrne paradigm was intended to study attraction under controlled conditions rather than in the realistic situation where multiple factors affect attraction, often in unknown ways. The effect of the Byrne paradigm, however, is to sacrifice *representativeness* and *naturalness,* and to raise questions regarding the generalizability of the findings outside of the laboratory.

There is further reason to doubt the importance of attitudinal or personality similarity in a variety of contexts in experiments conducted by other researchers. Consider the case where similarity does not have a positive value for the subject. Murstein (1971) found that, among pre-marital couples, the partner is perceived as less similar by low self-accepting persons as compared to the perceptions of high self-accepting couples. Apparently, the low self-accepting individuals seek someone with a somewhat different, more desirable, personality makeup than their own. To duplicate themselves in another would only multiply their woes.

Goldstein and Rosenfeld (1969) found that a preference for high similars on a personality inventory was greater for individuals who were insecure as compared to more secure subjects, who tended to select somewhat more dissimilar subjects as partners for a projected meeting. Overall, however, the subjects were more apt to choose similars than dissimilars. Earlier, Hoffman (1958) and Hoffman and Maier (1966) showed that in groups trying to achieve tasks in a competition-oriented setting, similarity was not important, but competence was very attractive.

Jellison and Zeisett (1969) demonstrated that the attractiveness of similarity fluctuates with the desirability of the similarity behavior and its commoness. When a desirable trait was shared with another, the other was liked more if the trait was uncommon than if it was common. However, if the trait shared was a negatively valued one, the other was liked more when a large percentage of the population possessed the trait than when only a few possessed it.

The findings of Novak and Lerner (1968) were rather similar. Their subjects learned that they were either very similar or dissimilar to another subject. When the partner was believed to be normal, interaction with him was desired more if he was believed to be similar rather than dissimilar. With a disturbed other, willingness to interact decreased with perceived similarity.

Last, Reitz (1968), working with a group of low self-esteem subjects found that, with desirable statements, only a trend existed to like strangers with increasing similarity. For undesirable statements, liking was strongly related to the perception of similarity in the stranger.

It is unfortunate that the use of the stranger as a constant in many of Byrne's investigations has not permitted the analysis of the difference in reinforcement strength between strangers and intimate associates for the same condition. Aronson (1970), reviewing the literature, concluded that strangers were liked more than associates when they produced positive evaluations of the subject. Presumably, the associate's positiveness is taken for granted so that the stranger offers the greatest opportunity for gain in esteem when he likes the subject. The "gain" explanation was also used to account for a finding of Jones, Bell and Aronson (quoted in Aronson, 1970) that a stimulus person who expressed dissimilar attitudes to those held by a subject but who, nevertheless, indicated that he liked the subject, would be liked better than one who also liked the subject but held attitudes similar to the subject.

I would suspect that further research will indicate that the strangers' greater reinforcement value is largely restricted to their novelty value, and that the tremendous reinforcement value of friends as contributors to an individual's homeostasis in his everyday environment has not been adequately represented in these studies. These results, nevertheless, indicate that the importance of similarity in attraction is highly specific to the situation.

The upshot of these studies is that if an individual possesses desirable traits he prefers to interact closely with someone whom he perceives as similar. If he does not possess desirable traits, he looks for a partner somewhat less similar to himself. In the case of interaction with a stranger, however, confidence in oneself leads to a greater interest in interaction with a somewhat dissimilar person. Anxiety about the self leads to a preference for more similar individuals. If similarity appears for undesirable traits, then the individual seeks to minimize his uniqueness as the possessor of these traits by perceiving their presence in others. The company of other possessors of negative traits becomes more desirable to the extent that they are normal people since, if normals possess them, they are really not as bad as they may seem at first sight.

The studies reviewed also tell us that attraction is a very complex phenomenon. Individuals behave differently with respect to attraction to a potential marriage partner and to a limited meeting with a stranger. It also makes a difference whether the other is normal or disturbed. Whether or not the traits perceived are desirable or undesirable also affects the similarity effect, as does the degree of self-acceptance of the subject.

There is yet another argument against the importance of similarity in attraction. Aronson and Worchel (1966) have argued that similarity is effective only because an individual, in the absence of other information (as in the bogus stranger paradigm), assumes that a person who holds an opinion similar to his own will like him. To test their belief the authors led students to believe that their partner in an experiment had attitudes similar or dissimilar to their own. Each of these two groups was further divided by the fact that the partner had allegedly stated that he either liked the subject very much or disliked him. The results indicated that the partner's liking or disliking of the subject affected his liking of the partner on a reciprocal basis. Attitudinal similarity, however, had no effect on liking.

Byrne and Griffitt (1966) concluded that Aronson and Worchel's failure to replicate Byrne's earlier findings was due to the restricted range of similarity and dissimilarity in their experiment. Extending this range, Byrne and Griffitt found both liking and similarity to be potent determinants of attraction, though, from their data, liking seemed clearly the stronger of the two determinants.

The comparative strengths of similarity and liking was reassessed in an experiment by Stalling (1970). His thesis was that similarity was a correlative of evaluative meaning, and that the latter rather than the former is responsible for the conditioning that takes place. He tested his thesis by employing trigrams (nonsense syllables of three letters) as the conditioned stimulus, with the unconditioned stimulus being represented by personality-trait adjectives. These adjectives were rated by the subject on evaluation and on similarity to himself. The words were selected on the dimensions of pleasantness-unpleasantness and similarity-dissimilarity to the subjects. The conditioning took place with the trigrams projected on a screen and the words (unconditioned stimuli) spoken one second after the onset of the trigram. An analysis of variance was computed for the mean evaluative ratings of the trigrams following conditioning. It revealed that evaluation was highly significant ($p < .005$), whereas similarity was not significant. Subjects, in short, liked the trigrams associated with the pleasant adjectives but made no distinction in their evaluation between similarity-dissimilarity when pleasantness-unpleasantness was held constant.

In like vein, McLaughlin (1970) failed to find a significant relationship between attraction and similarity when the self-descriptive adjectives used for the similarity dimension were partialled out by means of an analysis of covariance. Presumably, therefore, the stranger was liked because he was likeable, i.e., he chose likeable adjectives to describe himself just as the subject did in describing himself.

A last study by Murstein and Lamb (1971) offers a direct confrontation of similarity and liking with a group of subjects who had lived together anywhere from 4 months to $3\frac{1}{2}$ years. The subjects were 26 female residents of a girls' cooperative in which the nature of the living arrangements assured that the girls rapidly got to know each other. Using the Norman trait list (Norman, 1963), all subjects rated themselves according to a considerable number of variables of which those most pertinent to the present paper were self, ideal-self, ideal-friend, how they saw every other member of the house, and how they thought every other person saw them. In addition, they took the General Friendship Value Inventory, a series of values in friendship to be ranked in importance, developed earlier by Murstein. They also ranked every member of the house according to how much they liked them and estimated how much every other house member liked them.

A series of scores was generated from the data for each subject compared one at a time with every other subject. The scores included actual similarity of self-concepts, actual similarity of ideal-friend, actual validation of self-concept by other, actual ideal-self similarity, and actual similarity of General Friendship Value rankings. Also included were perceived validation of the self by other and perceived similarity to the ideal-self, self, and ideal-friend. Each of these scores was converted to ranks and correlated with liking for each of the subjects by the subject in question. Last, for each subject, his liking for every other subject was correlated with his perception of how much they liked him.

When various measures of actual similarity are observed, they prove to be uncorrelated with liking of the other (actual similarity of self, .00; actual similarity of ideal-friend, −.02; actual similarity of ideal-self, .01; actual similarity of general friendship values, −.03). The actual validation of the self by the other fared no better, (.05), and actual similarity as judged by peers showed only a nonsignificant trend, (.26). Even actual liking by the other, though significant, was only moderately associated with the subject's liking for other, .51 [the cutoff for significance is .32 ($p < .05$), and .44 ($p < .01$)].

If we turn to the perceived similarity scores (both perceptions stem from the same person), the picture becomes brighter. Perceived validation of the self shows a correlation of .34, and perceived similarity to the self shows a value of .37. The latter correlation is somewhat analogous to the Byrne test of similarity. In the Byrne paradigm the subject accurately perceives the objective similarity between himself and the stranger. In the Murstein and Lamb study, the subject perceives the similarity, but it seems reasonable to assume that, in the subject's mind at least, he is perceiving what he thinks is objectively true.

Going further, however, we note that perceived similarity to the ideal-self and ideal-friend showed correlations of .57 and .54 respectively, both considerably higher than perceived similarity to the self. Last, when actual liking was correlated with perceived liking, the resulting correlation was .80. This correlation does not tell us how much liking another influences perceived liking by the other as compared to the effect that perceiving another as liking oneself has on the other's actual liking of oneself. It does indicate, however, that in this "real life" study, similarity, though related to attraction, was not as important as a num-ber of other variables.

Conclusions Regarding the "Learning" Approach

Byrne's "law of interpersonal attraction" works very well within the restrictions of his paradigm. Though not a great deal of research as yet has occurred outside of the laboratory, the results so far indicate that similarity is of some importance as a *determinant of first impressions* so long as other possible determinants are either eliminated or mini-mized. When these other factors are allowed to operate as in a "real life" situation, the role of similarity is weakened but not eliminated.

The "bogus stranger" model's restriction on the operation of attrac-tion may be seen by use of an analogy. Suppose a wealthy sheik was seeking a fourth wife and asked the local mayor of a town to show him some of the fair beauties of the district. Suppose that the sheik was only allowed to observe the mammary development of these women, all other parts being covered and no verbal interaction being permitted. Under these conditions, it could be reliably demonstrated that whether or not the women were Muslims, or Christians, black or white, brunette or blond, fat or thin, wealthy or poor, toothless or toothsome, the ample, upstanding bosom would be preferred to the meager or bovine pendu-lant one in a majority of cases. One could probably construct a scale of an ideal breast and calculate choice as a function of departure from the ideal. There would of course be some error, as in this matter as well as others there is always the question of taste. Few would venture to pre-dict, however, that the woman chosen on the basis of breast would neces-sarily be chosen if the usual conditions of courtship were allowed to operate.

Among the other factors influencing attraction, therefore, are the kind of interaction (marriage, friendship, "one-night stand"), the self-perception of the individual, his ideals, the kind of information he receives about the other, the other's status, the effect of time, and the ability of the other to fulfill the role expectations of the subject and to permit him to fulfill his own role-expectations. As is illustrated in Chapter 6, it makes a difference whether we are talking of similarity of physical appearance, values, needs, or roles.

The evidence regarding the role of similarity in attraction, it should be stressed, does not pertain to Byrne's theory but to the importance of similarity within the theory as determined by his experiments. Byrne,

Griffitt, and Stefaniak have stated, "It is tentatively suggested that, with other variables held constant, the behavior of another individual is positively reinforcing to the extent that it is similar to one's own behavior" [1967, p. 83]. Our review casts considerable doubt on the validity of this suggestion when "likeableness" is partialled out of similarity. Attraction is too comprehensive a term to be a simple function of similarity unless unusual conditions surround the study of it. As Marlowe and Gergen note, "social attraction, like the concept of personality, has theoretical merit only as a generic term. Greater specificity regarding the exact nature of social attraction being studied in each individual instance is much in need if understanding of the relevant process is to be achieved" (1968, p. 622).

A last comment should be made about the relevance of classical conditioning to Byrne's model. Classical learning theorists may be perturbed over a condition of similarity serving as an unconditioned stimulus. In classical conditioning, the unconditioned response is supposed to occur rapidly and inevitably as a result of the appearance of the unconditioned stimulus. Obviously this does not occur in attraction because the unconditioned stimulus must first be searched for meaning. The context, status, self-concept, and other variables often play a mediating role before the response is made.

Whether one prefers a cognitive or learning model does not appear crucial to an appreciation of Byrne's work (see Chapter 4). The "law of interpersonal attraction" could function as well in a perceptual-cognitive framework as in a learning one. It seems necessary, however, to elaborate this model more fully if it is to be extended to the complexities encountered in "real life" studies.

Regardless of whether one finds this model useful, it can scarcely be questioned that the attempt to make "attraction" an integral part of the laws of behavior is a courageous and much needed effort. Certainly the work of Byrne, Lott, and their colleagues has elicited great interest and stimulated much research which seems likely to further our knowledge of such important but heretofore ignored topics as interpersonal attraction.

Exchange Theory

The Byrne paradigm mainly focused on the factors causing an individual to be attracted to another. Since in much of the research the "other" was a bogus stranger, it was not possible to study the interaction of the two and how it might influence attraction. A reinforcement theory came into focus a little over a decade ago, however, which deals with the transactions between members of a dyad and purports to explain social behavior including the kinds of interaction that lead to attraction. It is called exchange theory, and the individuals who did most to develop it in its current form were Thibaut and Kelley (1959), and Homans (1961).

The vocabulary of exchange theory is quite simple. Any behavior on the part of a person which provides a measure of need satisfaction to another person is said to be *rewarding* for the latter person. On the debit side of the ledger are *costs*. These are the unpleasant consequences which behavior may bring about. Suppose Johnny meets his friend Ephraim on his way home for supper. Johnny enjoys talking to Ephraim, and therefore the interaction is rewarding to Johnny. However, in talking to Ephraim, he overlooks the fact that he is supposed to be home for supper at 6:00 sharp. He arrives home at 6:10 to find an irritated family waiting at supper for him. This irritation is unpleasant and is a cost to him. Was it worthwhile to stop off? To determine the worth of the activity, the cost must be subtracted from the reward to yield the *outcome*. If the reward is greater than the cost, the outcome may be said to yield a *profit*. If the reward is outweighed by the cost it is said to yield a *loss*.

The cost does not have to be punishment or suffering of some kind. Homans notes that a cost can be having to forgo another pleasant experience. Suppose Johnny were on his way home to watch a football game on television. To the extent that he talked with Ephraim he would have to forgo some portion of the game as his cost.

Thibaut and Kelly introduce the comparison level to handle the problem of choosing between two rewarding or two costly alternatives. Attraction is dependent on the degree to which the profit is above a minimum level of expectation called a comparison level. This level is dependent on past experience, assessment of the current situation, and the general adaptation level of the individual at the present moment. By comparing his outcome against his comparison level, he decides to what degree he is satisfied or dissatisfied. Dissatisfaction is not invariably equivalent to a lack of attraction, however, for attraction also depends on the alternatives to the present situation; thus the individual also has a comparsion level for alternatives. In the case of our wife of an alcoholic husband, she might stay with her husband because, although her present situation is low on her comparison level, her comparison level for alternatives points to an even bleaker future if she leaves him.

The concept of exchange has furthered our understanding of behavior in several ways. In earlier days, for example, "popularity" was often treated as an attribute of an individual much as "good looks" is. Yet from the exchange point of view, popular individuals should be those who provide rewards for a great number of people. A study of Jennings (1950) verified this belief. Jennings was able to show the leaders in a girl's correctional institution performed more services for others than anyone else. They integrated others into activities, introduced new activities, and promoted acceptance of each other among the girls. Further, the leaders, by virtue of their self-control and ability to avoid manifesting anxiety or depression, minimized the cost to the other girls in interacting with them.

Elder (1969) has shown that subsequently mobile women were more likely to have been rated as attractive during their adolescence than non-mobile women of similar class origins. Such women engaged in less petting and coitus in high-school, since, presumably, their beauty was reward enough for their consorts. On the other hand, wives with more education than their spouses were more prevalent among the low-attractive women as compared to a high-attractive group, indicating that education was also a rewarding commodity though it appeared less potent in the exchange market than feminine pulchritude.

Skin color has long been highly differentiated in its rewarding power. Warner, Junker, and Adams (1941), and Udry, Bauman, and Chase (1971) showed that, among Negro women, lightness of color has been associated with upward mobility. Carter and Glick (1970), studying the 1960 census, noted support for the thesis "that a Negro who marries a white person tends to have superior qualities (specifically a higher education level) as compared with a Negro who married another Negro; and that a white person who married a Negro tends to have inferior qualities (educational level) as compared with a white person who marries another white person" (p. 127).

Propinquity also has been shown to function in exchange theory. Williams (1959) demonstrated that individuals who had friends outside of their community showed greater agreement with them on values than they did with friends within their community. The greater cost in traveling to see these friends was, as might be expected, offset by the greater rewards gained from interaction with them.

Similarity plays a more complex role in exchange theory. People of similar characteristics tend to congregate together. Students in a university tend to be of similar age, educational level, similar income, and to share many values. Similarity brings them together, because, from past experience, they and their parents have learned that similar backgrounds and values among interactants are highly rewarding. For one thing, similar orientations to life provide consensual validation that the individual is right in adhering to these values, since respected others also do so. Also, there is less cost in communicating with others since their values flow along similar lines.

In certain respects within the personality area, however, similarity is not necessarily rewarding. As we noted earlier, specific roles may require that two individuals play complementary roles rather than similar ones. It is for this reason that, from the exchange point of view, the strongest interpersonal relationships occur, not between the most similar persons, but between those with equal rewarding power even if the factors involved in these rewards are different for the partners.

In sum, exchange seems to pervade human behavior in many ways. In fact, several theorists (Gouldner, 1960; Lévi-Strauss, 1948) have suggested that reciprocity is the basic condition which makes civilization possible and keeps man from a perpetual series of savage brawls.

Despite the support that exchange theory has garnered, there are some reservations that can be raised to its formulation to this point. It seems to make of human behavior a rather selfish, egocentric, solipsistic endeavor. "What can you do for me?" seems to be the implicit motif of the theory, and the idea of spontaneous good works without assuring oneself of a profit in advance seems antithetical to the theory. The contemplation of billions of people assessing their profits and costs in relationships invokes the image of a capitalistic businessman more than that of a man who, according to the Bible, was created in God's image. Are we to conclude that Jesus, St. Francis of Assisi, Gandhi, and Albert Schweitzer were not the self-sacrificers they seemed to be but were secretly mulcting their fellow-man?

One way of accounting for altruistic behavior is by dividing rewards into two categories, intrinsic and extrinsic (Blau, 1964). Intrinsic rewards are those which come from an association itself. Extrinsic rewards are detachable from the association. The individual in the association is only a means to achieving the reward. A friend loved for himself is intrinsically gratifying, whereas a waiter who pleases a customer may do so only because the customer is a big tipper. These are extreme antipodal cases. In many associations the extrinsic and intrinsic rewards are subtly interwoven and difficult to separate. The professor gains extrinsic rewards in terms of salary from his teaching, but he also forms many enduring relationships of an intrinsic nature. Yet even if we confine ourselves to the category of ostensibly intrinsic relationships, the situation becomes complex when we ask *why* the association with others is rewarding for altruistic individuals. Clearly, they do not necessarily particularly enjoy the company of those whom they aid. It appears that their rewards are often internal—they come from the belief that they are living in accordance with their ideals; thus the individuals with whom they interact may be only tools or catalysts which make possible the reinforcements provided by the fulfillment of the ideal-self. How to weight these disparate rewards presents an awesome task for future research which will call for increasingly more specific predictions from exchange theory.

There is also some question as to whether exchange theory can embrace all kinds of behavior. It is clear that it applies readily to economic behavior. I buy a loaf of bread which I exchange for money. But, there are other systems which at first sight do not so readily fit into the exchange pattern. Consider a devoted couple married 18 years and still very much in "love" with each other. Are they still functioning in an exchange system? If we were to ask them about whether they were getting as much from their partner as they were giving, they would snort "more than I'm giving." In their second breath they would say that they are committed to each other and simply do not ever think of rewards and costs in their interaction with each other.

An exchange theorist might say that exchange theory influenced their behavior even if not consciously acknowledged; perhaps so. It remains incumbent on the exchange theorist, nevertheless, to tackle such difficult examples as "love systems" and "threat systems" and to prove that they can readily be encompassed by exchange theory (Boulding, 1962).

Blau (1964) has attempted an explanation of love, but his explanation, to this reader, seems vague and preoccupied with emphasizing the importance of regulating the supply and depth of affection so as not to depreciate its value by overgenerosity. There is scarcely a word paid to the value of the services performed, so intent is Blau in focusing on the transportation of the commodity. Neither he nor any other exchange theorist, however, has yet demonstrated that stable relationships are characterized by an equality of exchange of "love." More promising is the data on the role of exchange in attraction and in the early formation of relationships (see Chapter 6).

Homans' theory, according to Abrahamsson (1970), not only oversimplifies behavior but contains a certain conceptual turbidity which is masked over by Homan's great skill in verbal exposition. A reward, for example, cannot be distinguished operationally from a cost (a cost can be a reward foregone). Reward is sometimes utilized as an independent variable as in the formula, Reward $-$ Cost $=$ Outcome. At other times, reward becomes an intervening variable; thus from the knowledge of status of individuals, Homans predicts their esteem, presumably utilizing reward as an intervening but unmeasured variable.

There is something in exchange theory reminiscent of Freudian theory's facility of explaining away all theoretical problems without recourse to research. In therapy, if the client goes along with his analyst, all is well. If he does not, however, then he may be said to express "resistance." Such a system precludes the possibility of analysts erring and is doubtless gratifying to the analyst.

In exchange theory, Abrahamsson similarly points out that a careful reading of Homans suggests that it is rewarding to husband one's resources and not to husband one's resources, to be an egoist and to be an altruist, to achieve rewards by conforming and by not conforming. Further, there are rewards both when the price of a commodity is low and also when it is high, and it is rewarding to both concern oneself with status and not to concern oneself with it.

To be fair to Homans, it should be noted that any general theory must be applied in specific circumstances, and no theory can be broad enough to make predictions about every situation that might arise. Homans, and most of us, would probably agree that there are occasions when it is rewarding to be egotistical and other situations when it is rewarding not to be egotistical. The difficulty is that there is insufficient detail in Homans' theory to enable one to predict when one alternative will be chosen in preference to another.

In addition, Homans uses the analogy of economic exchange in arriving at his concept of satisfactions. But, "goods" in economics are readily quantifiable. The supply of utilities can be ascertained before the exchange takes place. Homans talks about the fact that when a supply of a utility is scarce, its value rises, but there is no comparable, simple way of measuring the supply of, for example, social approval and esteem.

In conclusion, exchange theory has already proved to be a provocative and research-stimulating theory. However, it appears to be at a crossroad. The homely, commonsense anecdote must be replaced by a more rigorous definition and classification of rewards and costs and a careful delineation of the conditions under which a given behavior serves as a reward or a cost. Last, the theory must restrict itself to certain kinds of interactions or, if it is to be maintained as a general theory of behavior, it must deal with such complex behaviors as commitment and threat in a more adequate fashion than heretofore.

BALANCE THEORY

First propounded by Fritz Heider (1946, 1958), balance theory has incurred an increasing amount of interest and research in recent years. As developed by Heider, balance theory concerns itself with attitudes and perceptions of a person (P) towards another person (O) and/or an object (X).* The two types of relations studied are *sentiment* and *unit*. A sentiment refers to the way P feels about or evaluates O or X, either positively or negatively. Neutrality of feeling plays no role, since it implies a lack of sentiment.

A unit relation involves a perceived unity of the two persons or of a person and object. When the perceived units and/or sentiments are perceived by P to exist without stress, they are said to be in a balanced state. A dyad is balanced, for example, if the relationship between P and O or P and X is either positive (+) or uniting (U), or is wholly negative (−) or nonuniting (non U). Imbalance occurs when relations of different signs occur. Some examples of balance would be: if P likes O (+) and believes that O likes him (+); if P likes X (+) and P owns X (U). However, if P likes O (+) but he believes O dislikes him (−), or, if P dislikes X (−) but P owns X (U), disharmony ensues.

In the case of the triad, just as in the dyad, all perceptions stem from P. In the triad there are three perceptions to consider: P→ O, P→ X, and O→ X. Note that this limitation excludes other possible perceptions such as, for example, O→ P. Balance occurs when all three of the relations are positive or two are negative and one is positive; thus if P likes O but dislikes X and believes O dislikes X, the situation is balanced. If P likes both O and X, but O dislikes X, the situation is imbalanced. The case of three negative relations is ambiguous and complicated and can be either balanced or imbalanced.

All cases of imbalance create stress. Whenever possible, therefore, P tends to resolve the stress by changing the character of the unit relation or the sign of the affect so as to restore balance; thus, if P likes O and X, but O dislikes X, P might try to get O to change his mind, or P might change his mind about either O or X.

Heider has done little research of an empirical nature with balance theory, but Newcomb, among others, has involved himself both in expanding the theory and testing Heiderian concepts. One change is to consider the perceptions of both P and O (collective system) in predicting balance or imbalance (Newcomb calls it degree of strain).

* Sometimes instead of an object there is a third person (Q).

It will be recalled that Heider's theory depends completely on the state of events as perceived by P only. In addition, Newcomb considers not only the sign of attraction (+ or −) but also the degree of intensity, something not considered by Heider.

There are even slight differences in defining balance. To Heider, negative attraction along with dissimilarity (unit relationship) is balanced, whereas to Newcomb such a relationship may be balanced or nonbalanced (the subject is indifferent or uncertain about the situation) (Newcomb, 1963). To Heider, negative attraction accompanied by similarity is necessarily imbalanced, whereas to Newcomb the situation is again either imbalanced or nonbalanced. Newcomb is able to make this distinction because, in his view, if we like O we assume O likes us, but disliking O does not lead us to assume that O dislikes us, particularly if we have never expressed this dislike. P's reaction, therefore, is influenced not only by the sign and unit relationship but by assumptions about the other's feelings, by object relevance, and by the degree of commitment to the activity.

Last, Newcomb's vocabulary is more familiar to psychologists than that of Heider and more akin to current theoretical thinking. Heider has been influenced by Gestalt thinking, as is evidenced by terminology like "harmonious," "fit," "unit relations," and "balance," which derive from a perceptual frame of reference. Newcomb utilizes learning theory as when he notes that when strain arises, communication may serve as an instrumental response in reducing this strain.

The research on balance theory has been summarized elsewhere (Insko, 1967; Kiesler, Collins, & Miller, 1969) and will not be reviewed here. Suffice it to note that the theory has obtained considerable support, but this has been mainly in simple, restricted, and rather artificial contexts. However, the theory's simplicity is now considered a weakness, and an increasing number of exceptions and complexities within it have recently been uncovered.

Difficulties with the Theory

1. One obvious difficulty with Heider's theory is its lack of quantitative metric. It is apparent that there are few people whom we totally like and few whom we totally dislike. Yet Heider provides no means of measuring degree of liking or degree of imbalance in his theory. It is possible, for example, that a situation may be imbalanced when P likes O and O likes P, if P likes O a great deal more than O likes him. The use of quantified scores would obviate this criticism but would at the

same time lead to theoretical difficulties as to what is a balanced state. If, for example, P likes O seven units worth and O likes P only four units worth, is the dyad balanced?

2. A related problem is the lack of conceptual clarification of liking. Some two thousand years ago Aristotle, in the *Nichomachean Ethics,* indicated that there are at least three reasons for liking someone: he is "good," "entertaining," or "useful." Many persons "like" oranges. They demonstrate this fact behaviorally by peeling the skin, discarding it, and consuming the remainder with relish. Fortunately, relatively few people are "liked" the way oranges are liked. It is probably true, nevertheless, that certain kinds of liking must have greater consequences for imbalance than other kinds, but this problem is not dealt with by Heider's theory.

3. Much the same criticism can be leveled at the concept of "unit relation." Saying that a person and an object "are perceived as belonging together" (Heider, 1958, p. 176) is extremely vague and of little heuristic value. Further, the absence of the unit relationship (U) and a negative relationship (−) are treated conceptually as being equal but, in fact, do not really seem equivalent; thus if Peter likes Mary and Peter likes horses, the fact that Mary does not own a horse would probably not cause a great deal of difficulty in the relationship. Cartwright and Harary (1956) have referred to such situations as vacuously balanced and found these situations to be intermediate in pleasantness between balanced and imbalanced states.

4. The role of the self-concept is scarcely considered. Heider does say that in positively balanced formulations he assumes that P has a positive regard for himself. But many of us are ambivalent about ourselves, liking ourselves in some ways, disliking ourselves in others. Balance theory does not adequately handle the interaction of self-concept and attitudes towards others, although Wiest (1965) has made a beginning here.

5. For Heider, an attitude towards an object has the same weight as an attitude towards a person. Yet research has not supported this aspect of the theory. A full discussion of this problem is given by Newcomb in Chapter 2 of this book.

6. The consequences of imbalance are not adequately considered. There is, for example, a great deal of variability among people in their tolerance of stress. For some persons, imbalance in interpersonal relationships is traumatic, whereas others find no difficulty in adjusting to the fact that another, for example, may not reciprocate their positive feelings.

7. The implication that balance is a good, pleasant, or desirable state does not completely jive with human experience. Individuals rarely seek Nirvana as a goal in life. Rather a moderate state of imbalance (level of activation) provides challenge for many. Such individuals may provoke imbalances for the pleasure of resolving them.

8. Evaluation of another apart from liking him is not considered. As Kiesler, Collins, and Miller (1969) point out, if P were to declare, "I love a whore and she loves me," most people would regard this dyad as imbalanced because of the low status of O. Heider could treat this event in either of two ways. He could say that P's love for O may be affected by her social status so that in effect he does not really love O. Or, he might say that P's personal affection for O was one aspect of their relationship. Another aspect of the relationship might be described as in Figure 1. This second aspect of the relationship is imbalanced because although P loves O, he also likes his reputation as a pillar of the community. Accordingly, he must visit O only by night so that she in no way is associated with his reputation. Ambivalence toward O, therefore, might be indicated by the fact that his total relationship with her involves both balanced and imbalanced components.

By resorting to such involved and complex ad hoc explanations, however, the main virtue of the theory's appeal, its simplicity, is sacrificed, and the impression is gained that any complex relationship will involve a gaggle of dyad and triad sketches.

9. The theory is vague about how imbalance may be resolved. In the case where P likes O, O likes X, and P dislikes X, the theory acknowledges that P may change his liking of O, or of X, or he might decide that O doesn't really like X. Another way of resolving the imbalance would be to redefine the relationship with O so as to exclude any feeling on his part about X as it relates to the relationship. The theory, however, provides no way of predicting which of these alternatives is apt to be used.

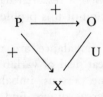

FIG. 1. *Imbalanced situation arising because O (a whore) is united with X (P's reputation as a clean, upstanding pillar of society).*

10. No consideration is given to the fact that knowledge of certain attitudes leads to the assumption of other attitudes, and that these assumptions do not follow a symmetrical course. Price, Harburg, and Newcomb (1966) provide a case in point in their basic finding that in a three-person situation involving P, O, and Q, when P (the actual subject) liked O, the various triads as in Table 1 were either balanced or imbalanced in accordance with the theory. However, when P disliked O, the balanced situations were not always agreeable, and the imbalanced situation was not always disagreeable.

An objection could be made to the equation of balance with agreeableness, but for the sake of argument let us assume that the two are conceptually very similar. How then to account for the results? Fortunately, additional information by the authors provides the answer. When P was asked to report how his best friend (P $\xrightarrow{+}$ O) felt about him, 98 per cent reported that they were liked in return by O; thus when P liked O, he almost automatically assumed O liked him. When P actively disliked another person, however (P $\xrightarrow{-}$ O), assumptions of reciprocity did not automatically follow; thus 27 per cent of the Ps judged that their dislike of O we reciprocated, but 26 per cent believed that O liked them, and 47 per cent were uncertain.

It is also noteworthy that when "best friend" was ranked on a ten-point scale of liking, he received a mean value of 8.3, whereas a "strongly disliked" person received a mean value of 5.5. There is, apparently, a strong feeling of positivity towards our fellow-man (at least in ratings of fellow college students), and even "strongly disliked" persons elicit only mild dislike or neutrality when the affect about them is scaled.

Putting all of the evidence together, we conclude that different assumptions of another's feelings may be associated with liking him as compared to disliking him, and "imbalance" in the latter becomes ambivalent rather than unpleasant; thus, as Table 1 shows, balanced states such as the +,+,+ of A are much more attractive as compared to the balanced state —,—,+ of G. However, there is even a substantial difference between two identically signed balanced (B and G) or imbalanced states (C and E). The comparison of D and E illustrates yet another asymmetry of expectation, in that it is more difficult to believe that a person whom we like will choose a disliked other (situation C). than it is to believe that a disliked other will choose a liked other (situation E).

11. Balance theory does not handle sequence effects within its theorectical framework. The fact, for example, that a person who formerly

TABLE 1. *Percentage of Subjects Responding with Varying Signs of Affect to Eight Basic Situations*

Type of Situation	Sign of Affect		
	− (Uneasy)	N (Neutral)	+ (Pleasant)
A.[a] $\quad$ p—+→o, p—+→q, q—+→o	6	7	87
B.[a] $\quad$ p—+→o, p—−→q, q—−→o	5	6	89
C. $\quad$ p—+→o, p—+→q, q—−→o	89	0	11
D. $\quad$ p—+→o, p—−→q, q—+→o	84	8	8
E. $\quad$ p—−→o, p—+→q, q—+→o	65	15	22
F. $\quad$ p—−→o, p—−→q, q—−→o	17	38	45
G.[a] $\quad$ p—−→o, p—+→q, q—−→o	43	22	35
H.[a] $\quad$ p—−→o, p—−→q, q—+→o	28	39	33

[a] Balanced situations, all others being imbalanced.

SOURCE: Adapted from Price, Harburg, and Newcomb, 1966, p. 266.

disliked another now likes him is scored only as a + just as the fact that a person who formerly liked another and still does is also marked +. Yet, Aronson and Linder (1965) reported that in the former case, the conversion of a negatively attracted person to the positive side of the ledger made the individual more attractive than the "faithful" individual who always liked the other.

In conclusion, balance theory seems valuable in that some of its general tenets seem correct and because it has generated a great deal of research. Like most simplistic theories, however, its brevity and parsimony have turned out to be its "Achilles heel" as exception after exception is being inscribed in the research literature.

OTHER THEORIES OF ATTRACTION

There are several other theories of attraction that appear in the book, but no preparatory exposition seems necessary to aid in digesting the subsequent chapters which touch upon them. The theory of marital choice which I have formulated, called Stimulus-Value-Role, is a combination of a longitudinal series of courtship stages and exchange theory. The latter has already been described, and the sequences of courtship stages is fully expounded in Chapter 6. Winch's "complementary needs" theory is likewise described in Chapter 6. The Walster theory of "passionate love" is based on Schacter's theory of "emotional state." The theory is relatively simple conceptually and is fully described in her article so that it needs no elaboration here.

It is my hope that this brief preamble has whetted the reader's appetite for the more specialized accounts which follow. Bon appetit!

REFERENCES

Abrahamsson, B. Homans on exchange: Hedonism revived. *American Journal of Sociology*, 1970, *76*, 273-285.

Aronson, E. Some antecedents of interpersonal attraction. In W. J. Arnold, and D. Levine (eds.), *Nebraska symposium on motivation 1969.* Lincoln, Nebraska: University of Nebraska Press, 1970. 143-173.

Aronson, E., & Linder D. Gain and loss of esteem as determinants of interpersonal attractiveness. *Journal of Experimental Social Psychology,* 1965, *1,* 156-171.

Aronson, E., & Worchel, P. Similarity versus liking as determinants of interpersonal attractiveness. *Psychonomic Science,* 1966, *5,* 157-158.

Backman, C. W., & Secord, P. F. Liking, selective interaction, and misperception in congruent interpersonal relations. *Sociometry,* 1962, *25,* 321-335.

Blau, P. M. Exchange and power in social life. New York: Wiley, 1964.

Boulding, K. E. Two critiques of Homans' social behavior in its elementary forms: An economist's view. American Journal of Sociology, 1962, 67, 458-461.

Byrne, D. Attitudes and attraction. In L. Berkowitz, (ed.), Advances in experimental social psychology. New York: Academic Press, 1969. 35-85.

Byrne, D., Baskett, G. D., & Hodges, L. Behavioral indicators of interpersonal attraction. Paper presented at The Psychonomic Society, St. Louis, November, 1969.

Byrne, D., Bond, M. H., & Diamond, M. J. Response to political candidates as a function of attitude similarity-dissimilarity. Human Relations, 1969, 22, 251-262.

Byrne, D., & Clore, G. L. A reinforcement model of evaluative response. Personality: An International Journal, 1970, 1, 103-128.

Byrne, D., Ervin, C. R., & Lamberth, J. Continuity between the experimental study of attraction and real-life computer dating. Journal of Personality and Social Psychology, 1970, 16, 157-165.

Byrne, D., & Griffitt, W. Similarity versus liking A clarification. Psychonomic Science, 1966, 6, 295-296.

Byrne, D., & Nelson, D. Attraction as a linear function of proportion of positive reinforcements. Journal of Personality and Social Psychology, 1965, 1, 659-667.

Carter, H., & Glick, P. C. Marriage and divorce: A social and economic study. Cambridge: Harvard University Press, 1970.

Cartwright, D., & Harary, F. Structural balance: A generalization of Heider's theory. Psychological Review, 1956, 63, 277-293.

Day, B. R. A comparison of personality needs of courtship couples and same sex friendship. Sociology and Social Research, 1961, 45, 435-440.

Efran, M. G. Visual interaction and interpersonal attraction. Unpublished doctoral dissertation, University of Texas, 1969.

Elder, Jr., G. H. Appearance and education in marriage mobility. American Sociological Review, 1969, 34, 519-533.

Fiedler, F. E. The psychological distance dimension in interpersonal relations. Journal of Personality, 1953, 22, 142-150.

Goldstein, J. W., & Rosenfeld, H. M. Insecurity and preference for persons similar to oneself. Journal of Personality, 1969, 37, 253-268.

Golightly, C., & Byrne, D. Attitude statements as positive and negative reinforcements. Science, 1964, 146, 798-799.

Gouldner, A. W. The norm of reciprocity: A preliminary statement. American Sociological Review, 1960, 25, 161-178.

Griffitt, W. B. Interpersonal attraction as a function of self-concept and personality similarity-dissimilarity. Journal of Personality and Social Psychology, 1966, 4, 581-584.

Heider, F. Attitudes and cognitive organization. Journal of Psychology, 1946, 21, 107-112.

Heider, F. The psychology of interpersonal relationships. New York: Wiley, 1958.

Hoffman, L. R. Similarity of personality: A basis for interpersonal attraction? Sociometry, 1958, 21, 300-308.

Hoffman, L. R., & Maier, N. R. F. An experimental reexamination of the similarity-attraction hypothesis. *Journal of Personality and Social Psychology,* 1966, *3,* 145-152.

Homans, G. C. *Social behavior: Its elementary forms.* New York: Harcourt, Brace, & World, 1961.

Insko, C. A. *Theories of attitude change.* New York: Appleton-Century-Crofts, 1967.

Izard, C. Personality similarity and friendship. *Journal of Abnormal and Social Psychology,* 1960, *61,* 47-51. (a)

Izard, C. Personality similarity, positive effect, and interpersonal attraction. *Journal of Abnormal and Social Psychology,* 1960, *61,* 484-485. (b)

Izard, C. Personality similarity and friendship: A follow-up study. *Journal of Abnormal and Social Psychology,* 1963, *66,* 598-600.

Jellison, J. M., & Zeisset, P. T. Attraction as a function of the commonality and desirability of a trait shared with another. *Journal of Personality and Social Psychology,* 1969, *11,* 115-120.

Jennings, H. H. *Leadership and isolation* (2nd ed.). New York: Longmans, Green & Co., 1950.

Kiesler, C. A., Collins, B. E., & Miller, N. *Attitude change.* New York: Wiley, 1969.

Lévi-Strauss, C. *Les structures élémentaires de la parenté.* Paris: Presses Universitaires, 1949.

Lott, A. J., & Lott, B. E. Group cohesiveness as interpersonal attraction: A review of relationships, with antecedent and consequent variables. *Psychological Bulletin,* 1965, *64,* 259-309.

Marlowe, D., & Gergen, K. Personality and social interaction. In G. Lindzey and E. Aronson (eds.), *Handbook of social psychology, Vol. 3.* Reading, Mass.: Addison-Wesley, 1968. Pp. 595-655.

McLaughlin, B. Similarity, recall, and appraisal of others. *Journal of Personality,* 1970, *38,* 106-116.

Miller, N., Campbell, D. T., Twedt, H., & O'Connell, E. J. Similarity, contrast and complementarity in friendship choice. *Journal of Personality and Social Psychology,* 1966, *3,* 3-12.

Murstein, B. I. Self-ideal-self discrepancy and the choice of marital partner. *Journal of Consulting and Clinical Psychology,* 1971, *35.* In press.

Murstein, B. L., & Lamb, J. Correlates of liking at a woman's college cooperative house. Unpublished manuscript, Connecticut College, 1971.

Newcomb, T. M. *The acquaintance process.* New York: Holt, Rinehart, & Winston, 1961.

Newcomb, T. M. Stabilities underlying changes in interpersonal attraction. *Journal of Abnormal and Social Psychology,* 1963, *66,* 376-386.

Norman, W. T. Toward an adequate taxonomy of personality attributes. Replicated factor structure in peer nomination personality ratings. *Journal of Abnormal and Social Psychology,* 1963, *66,* 574-583.

Novak, D. W., & Lerner, M. J. Rejection as a consequence of perceived similarity. *Journal of Personality and Social Psychology,* 1968, *9,* 147-152.

Price, K. O., Harburg, E., & Newcomb, T. M. Psychological balance in situations of negative and interpersonal attitudes. *Journal of Personality and Social Psychology*, 1966, *3*, 265-270.

Reader, N., & English, H. B. Personality factors in adolescent friendships. *Journal of Consulting Psychology*, 1947, *11*, 212-220.

Reilly, M. A., Commins, W. D. and Stefic, E. C. The complementarity of personality needs in friendship choice. *Journal of Abnormal and Social Psychology*, 1960, *61*, 292-294.

Reitz, W. E. Interpersonal attraction in low self-esteem persons. Paper presented at the Canadian Psychological Association Meetings, Calgary, June, 1968.

Stalling, R. B. Personality similarity and evaluative meaning as conditioners of attraction. *Journal of Personality and Social Psychology*, 1970, *14*, 77-82.

Thibaut, J. W., & Kelley, H. H. *The social psychology of groups.* New York: Wiley, 1959.

Udry, J. R., Bauman, K. E., & Chase, C. A. Skin color, status, and mate selection. *American Journal of Sociology*, 1971, *76*, 722-733.

Warner, W. L., Junker, B. H., & Adams, W. A. *Color and human culture.* Washington, D. C.: American Council on Education, 1941.

Williams, R. M. Jr. Friendship and social values in a suburban community: An exploratory study. *Pacific Sociological Review*, 1959, *2*, 3-10.

Wiest, W. M. A quantitative extension of Heider's theory of cognitive balance applied to interpersonal perception and self-esteem. *Psychological Monographs*, 1965, No. 14 (Whole No. 607).

2

Dyadic Balance as a Source of
Clues About Interpersonal Attraction

Theodore M. Newcomb

I happen to believe that interpersonal attraction is something that permeates a very great deal of human behavior, directly or indirectly. If we really understood it, we'd be very wise indeed about many if not most facets of the human condition, and thus we'd be better social scientists. This bias of mine is rooted in what I consider the elementary fact that attitudes toward people are rarely divorced from attitudes toward whatever objects, events, and concerns we have in common with them. Since the reverse is also true, I think of these matters in system terms: the two kinds of orientations are interdependent; change in either serves to instigate change in the other, and resistance to change in either tends to solidify and perpetuate the other. Thus I view influences toward change as impinging not just on single, insulated attitudes, but on systems of them.

My emphasis on attitudes, by the way, as distinguished from behavior, is not intended to beg the question about causal relations between the two. For present purposes I shall simply assume that here again the casual arrow can point in either direction. Attitude and behavior also have system-like relations.

Systems, of course, have properties of their own. It is the system property of *balance* that presently interests me. The term itself is simply a metaphor that implies stability, whereas imbalance implies relative susceptibility to change—change anywhere in the system provided only that it tends to achieve or restore a balanced state. The latter, according to theories as disparate as Heider's and Festinger's, is considered balanced, or relatively stable, simply because it is psychologically preferred. Imbalanced states are, by assumption, uncomfortable—tension-like, in the Lewinian sense.

But balance theory, in all its several versions, is itself a bit unstable. The literature is full of research findings that report exceptions to the general principles, or that simply fail to replicate previous findings. My concern in this paper is to examine some of these discrepancies in one limited area of balance theory—that which I have labeled "interpersonal." That is, I shall be concerned only with dyadic attraction in the context of attitudes toward other entities—objects, ideas, or persons—toward which both members of the dyad have some sort of orientation.

My intended concern, in what follows, is not to argue the supremacy of forces toward balance in interpersonal attraction, but rather to ask whether research findings concerning balance, as of now, are in any ways illuminating about social psychological processes. I shall be dealing in the main with two kinds of anomalies or deviations from theoretical predictions that have sometimes been deduced from the hypotheses of balance theory.

THE SPECIAL CASE OF NEGATIVE ATTRACTION

Heider, as everyone knows, was the first systematic formulator of the principles that apply to the experiencing of "separate entities" together in terms of balance (1944, 1946). "The concept of balanced state," he wrote in 1958, "designates a situation in which the perceived units [entities experienced as belonging together] and the experienced sentiments [attitudes, in the more common usage] co-exist without stress; there is thus no pressure toward change, either in the cognitive organization or in the sentiment" (p. 176). All subsequent treatments of the general problem, including my own, have adopted some form of this assumption.

Heider's formal statements of the conditions of balance include the following: "A triad is balanced when all three of the relations among O (the focal person), P (a second person), and X (an entity toward which O assumes that both have a relation) are positive or when two of the relations are negative and one is positive. Imbalance occurs when two of the relations are positive and one is negative. The case of the three negative relations is somewhat ambiguous . . ." (1958, pp. 202-3). It has become common practice (in spite of Heider's misgivings about the all-negative triad) to phrase the formula as follows: the triad is balanced if the algebraic product of the three signs is positive, and imbalanced if the product is negative.

For present purposes I want to point out two general features of Heider's position. First, relations among cognized entities that are susceptible to forces of balance are subject to a kind of equifinality—that is, insofar as they are presently in balance they tend to remain as they are, and insofar as they are not they tend to change toward balance. Second, different combinations of signs of relations among P, O, and X can be balanced or imbalanced by varying locations of signs; it is sheerly the *number* of plus and minus signs that determines balance or imbalance and not their *placement*, as between P and O, or P and X, or O and X. Thus, *any* set of two pluses and one minus, for example, is equivalent to any other set of two pluses and a minus.

It is this last assumption that I have questioned, first on theoretical grounds (1968; see also Price, Harburg and Newcomb, 1966). I see but one reason, a priori, for assuming that the psychological processes involved in a person's attraction to another person and in his attitude toward impersonal objects may be considered identical. The case for that assumption is still weaker as between P/O and O/X—that is, a person's (P) attraction to another person (O) and his judgment of the other's attitude (O) toward an impersonal object (X). That single reason is the neatness, or elegance, of the formulation, which can be generalized in terms of the algebraic product of three plus-or-minus signs. The history of science is studded with instances of premature closure in response to the lure of simple formulae.

Here is an important problem involved in the assumption of the equivalence of plus signs, or of minus ones, regardless of their placement in the triad. Person P's attraction to another person, O, is influenced by his assumptions about O's reciprocation of P's attraction. It seems likely that a plus P/O is stronger if P perceives positive reciprocation from O than if he assumes negative reciprocation. (I do not assume that the "causal" relation is exclusively from perceived O/P to P/O, but only that the influence, often if not always, is included in the relationship.) At any rate, the empirical evidence known to me amply supports this expectation. But assumptions of attraction toward oneself simply do not apply to impersonal objects of attitudes; they do not reciprocate one's attraction. From this I infer that a + P/O is not psychologically equivalent to a + P/X, and that there is a loss or distortion of information if one assumes that they are interchangeable—in the manner, say, of redwood trees: if you've seen one of them you've seen them all.

Since this point (to me, at least) seems evident, one may wonder why Heider and others who have worked with triads have ignored it. Basically, the reason has to do with adaptations that a person makes when he's in a state of imbalance. To take a homely example, if a person discovers that an admired friend disagrees with him on what he regards as an important issue (an imbalanced state of two pluses and one minus), he has at least these alternative ways of restoring balance: he can change P/O (thus disliking the friend), he can change P/X (reversing his own attitude), or he can change O/X (by convincing himself that his friend's attitude has been reversed). If we assume that each of these changes results in a balanced state (each changed state has one plus and two minuses), then we have assumed that it's the number and not the placement of signs that matters. If balance theory has any theoretical utility, it is precisely along these lines of predicting both those conditions under which change will occur, and also the general direction of those changes. For such reasons Heider and others have had to define triadic balance in terms of numbers of signs.

But any set of assumptions is bought at a price, which in this instance has been the implicit assumption that any combination of balanced signs is equivalent to any other balanced combination. I think this implication is both erroneous and unnecessary. I even believe Heider would agree, and here are my reasons.

Balance theory, like any other theory of dynamics, has to do with stability and change—after all, the principal characteristic of balanced states is that they are free from forces toward change. My point is that certain kinds of Heiderian balance are less stable than others, and are in fact accompanied by certain forces to change. In particular, I have in mind the balanced state whose single negative relation is P/O—the attraction bond.

My interest in this special problem began in the usual way—i.e., by noting apparently systematic differences between Heider-balanced triads in which P/O was plus and those in which it was minus. Price, Harburg and I (1966) therefore constructed a questionnaire in which all possible combinations of triad-signs were systematically varied (we used a third person, Q, described only as someone liked or disliked by P or by O, rather than an impersonal X). Our suspicions were strikingly supported: mean scores of "unpleasantness" when P/O was positive were consistently very low for balanced and *very* high for imbalanced triads. When P/O was negative, however, unpleasantness ratings were much less extreme in both balanced and imbalanced triads, and the range of scores within each category was much greater; moreover, we found the proportions of neutral responses (neither pleasant nor unpleasant) to be much higher than when P/O was positive. We interpreted these findings in terms of the arousal, under conditions of negative P/O, of forces other than those toward balance. These included uncertainty about reciprocation of O's attraction toward P and Q; ambivalence with regard to desire for both positive and negative reciprocation from a disliked person; and the lesser degree of "engagement" vis-a-vis a disliked person (e.g., "What do I care about a person whom I don't value?").

All of the other studies known to me that use methods similar to these support the following generalizations.* (The "ease of learning" procedures employed by Zajonc and Burnstein, 1965a and 1965b, provide an interesting exception; see my discussion of this, 1968.)

1. Responses to Heider-balanced triads that include a negative P/O differ markedly from those in which P/O is positive.
2. Ratings of unpleasantness, or "willingness to change signs," when P is negative are intermediate between Heider-balanced and Heider-imbalanced triads when P/O is positive.
3. Mean score differences between Heider-balanced and Heider-imbalanced triads when P/O is negative are very small, and of dubious significance.
4. Mean score differences between Heider-balanced and Heider-imbalanced triads (regardless of sign of P/O) are much smaller than differences between balanced and imbalanced triads when P/O is positive.

These findings lead me to ask, "What is to be said about a category system, one or more of whose categories include a subset that, empirically, resembles subsets of another category more closely than it resembles other subsets within the same category? At any rate I have been led to conclude that, in terms of psychological processes, Heider's balance-imbalance category ignores some very important differences. The crucial finding here, based on several studies, is that Heider-balanced triads including negative P/O differ more from Heider-balanced triads includ-

---

* These include Jordan (1953), Rodrigues (1966, 1967), Morrissette (1958), Hershkowitz (1966), and Steiner and Spaulding (1966); the last of these provides only partial support.

ing positive P/O than they differ from *any* Heider-imbalanced triads—
i.e., in respect to various ratings of tension (Newcomb, 1968, pp. 38, 39).

I have therefore proposed (1968) a distinction between positively
balanced, positively imbalanced, and nonbalanced states. The last of
these include all triads in which P/O is negative. In all studies known
to me that report data for all possible combinations of signs within
triads, responses to situations that I consider nonbalanced are intermediate between the others, and the negative P/O triads, considered
balanced by Heider, resemble the imbalanced situations more closely
than the positively balanced (by my classification).

Now let me return to my initial question: what is to be learned from
these kinds of analyses? I think the answers go something like this. First,
Heider's formulation is something like the pre-Newtonian ideas of
planetary orbits: since the circle is "perfect," as any other form of orbit is
not, then it must be assumed that God would not have planned anything
less perfect than a circular planetary orbit. It took empirical data to
dislodge this assumption, and with its dislodgement came much improved
understanding of the laws of thermodynamics. Second, in terms of my
specific and distinctly limited problem, perhaps such revisions as I have
offered to Heider's formulations may help to confirm such added complexities as the following. That particular subspecies of attitude that we
know as interpersonal attraction is peculiarly sensitive to the input of
new information—to wit, information about how the recipient of one's
attraction reciprocates what he receives from oneself. This does not
necessarily imply that persons, as objects of attitudes, are more fluid than
impersonal objects, information input about many of which is also in a
state of flux. It does imply, however, that humans are more apt to be
sensitively attuned to feedback from persons than from nonpersons. And
this, in turn, most surely stems from the fact that our very humanness
depends upon this kind of feedback. Any theory, no matter how "elegant," that ignores this basic fact of human life is sure to need revision.

THE IDENTIFICATION OF BALANCE-RELEVANT OBJECTS

Let me introduce this problem by way of an illustration of a commonly asserted limitation of the applicability of balance theory. "This
is the case of a Romantic Triangle: Joe loves Ann; Ann loves Harry. . . .
Does it follow that Joe likes Harry . . .? Intuition and experience clearly
suggest that under these circumstances Joe would not like Harry"

(Abelson, in Abelson et al, 1968, p. 127). A few pages away, in the book from which this is quoted, I have considered the same issue, in the following manner.

If the X in this situation is taken to be simply "Harry is a person of admirable qualities," the triad is balanced for Joe, since he likes Ann and agrees with her in admiring Harry. So far, no contradiction between theory and everyday observation. But the fact is that Joe views Harry not just as a likeable person but also as a potential competitor. Joe is not likely, in his search for balance, to go to such lengths as to convince himself that Harry is only a fine person and not at all a competitor. Rather, the salient triad for Joe will consist of himself as lover, Harry as a competitor, and Ann as his and his only. Such a triad is imbalanced— two pluses (Joe's attraction toward Ann and Ann's toward Harry) and one minus (Joe's toward Harry, who is a threat to Joe). And this too corresponds to everyday experience.

Abelson concludes quite simply that "Joe would not like Harry," period, whereas I maintained (in the book to which he and I both contributed chapters) that "in instances like this one there are both aspects [of the P/O relation] that induce balance . . . and other aspects that induce imbalance" (Abelson, et al, eds., 1968, p. 48, p. 127). He goes on to suggest that my "reinterpretation requires certain seemingly arbitrary semantic contortions in order to make matters come out right." This, as it happens, was exactly the opposite of what I was trying to say, and so I can only conclude that I wrote very badly. You will therefore understand my interest in presenting the issue now, as I really intend it to be.

No one interested in balance theory has ever asserted that balance is the rule, always and everywhere. If this were the case, there would be nothing to study, and people like me would have nothing to do. The trick is to discover the conditions under which forces toward balance predominate over other forces—induced by rivalry and competition, for example—and those under which they do not. The triadic situation of Joe, Harry, and Ann is clearly of the latter kind, where strong motivational states, combined with a recognition of reality combine to override forces toward balance.

My point was intended to be simply that even situations of this kind can be analyzed *in terms of* balance, with the consequence that perhaps something can be learned from the analysis. What emerged from my own "reinterpretation" of the case of Joe, Harry, and Ann can be summarized as follows: The situation, clearly imbalanced as described, *could* become balanced for Joe if something changed so that he no longer perceived Harry as a threat (e.g., either his own love for Ann changes to "mere liking," or he perceives Harry's attraction for Ann to have changed in the same way; Joe would doubtless prefer the latter kind of change). If some such change does not occur, the situation remains imbalanced— and, by definition, relatively unstable. Two things can therefore be said about it: first, that in the long run some change in the direction is *likely* to be made—though this is not certain, because one way of adapting to imbalance is to learn to live with it (after all, practically all psychological predictions are stated in probabilistic terms). And second, until and unless such changes occur, forces toward balance remain experienced in the form of strains or tensions.

Now I turn to the question of pay-offs from this kind of analysis. What can it teach us about the psychology of interpersonal attraction? For me it has begun with the realization that the "common object of orientation" (the X or the Q) is not necessarily what it first seems to be. X $\neq$ X. Insofar as two persons' attraction toward each other is supported by forces toward balance, any one of their presumably common attitude-objects can be viewed in different ways. In cases like that of Joe, Harry, and Ann, the differences have to do with different role perceptions. Joe as a male friend $\neq$ Joe as a competitive suitor. It is likely, as a matter of fact, that this stricture applies to many if not most competitive situations. I happen to be a social psychologist who cannot get along without certain kinds of role-conceptions. Though I have long held this point of view, I have not always realized the necessity of taking role distinctions into account as I pursued my interests in interpersonal balance theory.

Of course such considerations raise questions about what determines a person's selective perception of another person as taking one role rather than another. I shall briefly note only two points. 1) Very often P is aware of more than one role relationship, with the possible consequences for him of conflict, ambiguity, or uncertainty. Such, indeed, is the nature of the common human condition. 2) In any here-and-now situation, P is apt to view O in one of these multiple possible roles. His selection among alternative perceptions is determined by habit, by motivation of the moment, and by "reality" (as distinct from autism), particularly as signaled by present or recent behavior of O. There is nothing new about all this: interpersonal attraction, like other psychological processes, is a resultant of just such influences. My principal point, however, is that many instances of interpersonal attraction, as viewed from the perspective of balance theory, are complicated by the possibility of multiple and even conflicting role relationships. Hence the researcher in this area cannot assume that he knows what is "the real" relationship (even in an experimentally contrived investigation), but rather must be alert to other possibilities. Indeed, the fact of unexpected findings may provide a clue that differing kinds of role relationships have been assumed by respondents. Perhaps there is a unique triad for each kind of role relationship.

CONVERGENCES OF THE TWO PROBLEMS

Let me note a point at which my two problems converge. I reported first that predictions derived from "classical" balance theory are often not well supported in the case of negative interpersonal attraction. The finding seems to me to inhere particularly in conflicts and uncertainties in the respondent's assumptions about reciprocated attraction from the disliked person to himself. Then I went on to question simple predictions to the effect that if each of two persons is positively attracted to a third, then the first two persons should in all circumstances be positively attracted to each other. Here, as elsewhere, a contra-predicted finding should lead to examination of the bases for one's prediction. My own re-examination of certain competitive relationships led me to a closer scrutiny of the alternative ways in which one's own relationship to another may be viewed—in particular, varying role relationships.

What these two complications of interpersonal balance theory have in common is not just that empirical tests of a prediction from a formal theory have in both cases failed, in whole or in part, to correspond with the predictions. Nor am I interested in the possibilities of "saving the theory" by complicating it to fit the findings—though I believe that nearly every theory, as first formulated, has in all areas of science been subject to later modifications as its implications come to be tested under an increasingly wide range of conditions. What does interest me is the possibility—and, if one starts with a theory already known to have a good deal of merit, even the likelihood—that by examining discrepancies from existing, theoretically based predictions, one can gain further understanding of the processes whose outcomes the theory is designed to explain.

And this behooves me, I guess, to say something about the psychological processes that I believe I understand better now than before I examined some discrepancies. Since what I have learned from discrepancies about positive and negative attraction and from discrepancies in competitive situations have a point of convergence, I shall dwell only on that point. They both have to do with conflicts, ambivalences, ambiguities, or uncertainties about P/O relationships.

As to the distinction between positive and negative P/O, let me start with a single assumption—that no matter what one's level of self-esteem, or how much ambivalence one has about it, the self is always a positive value, and, with rare exceptions, support or enhancement of that value is welcomed. When one's own positive attraction toward someone is viewed as reciprocated, a triad consisting of P (as source of attitude), O (the other person), and X (self as object) is balanced (all pluses). But if P sees his own positive attraction to O as negatively reciprocated, then that triad is imbalanced and unwelcome. Thus to the tension of imbalance is added the ambivalence and uncertainty that goes with hoping for one thing while suspecting another. No wonder that measures of unpleasantness, or of desire to change triadic relations, are higher when P/O is negative than when it is positive. With this "discovery" I learn—or should I say relearn?—that the strong and virtually never-flagging motivation toward self-esteem can never be assumed to be absent from the dynamics of interpersonal attraction.

A similar "intrusion" of conflicts and uncertainties, also not accounted for by the three dyadic signs, appears in my analysis of a competitive situation. Joe faces a conflict between his role relationship to Harry as friend and his relationship as competitor. The likable characteristics that Joe attributes to Harry in the role of friend are not necessarily erased by the role relationship of threatening competitor; it's only that the latter takes precedence, since stronger motives than those toward balance become engaged, in spite of the ambivalence. In several of my publications (e.g., 1953, 1961) I have tried to account for the subordina-tion of forces toward balance under conditions of competition by posit-ing, as one of the parameters of force toward balance, "joint relevance," a notion something like "common fate." That is, if a given object or event has differential impacts upon O and P, there is no reason why different attitudes toward it should lead to the tensions of imbalance. In the case of Joe versus Harry for Ann, they are subject to not only differen-tial impacts, but opposed ones from the same event (e.g., "if he wins, I lose"); there is opposed rather than joint relevance. There are good rea-sons for introducing the notion of common fate (which also applies to situations other than competitive ones), but for present purposes I prefer to emphasize the aspects of conflict, ambivalence, and their attendant un-certainty. In any case, my present analysis of a competitive situation has not taught me anything about common and opposed fates, but I think I have learned something about the gray areas where attraction toward another person is not the result of a unanimous, internal vote.

In situations of negative attraction, enough tension is aroused so that classically balanced and certain imbalanced triads are hardly distinguish-able. In competitive situations, imbalance is tolerated if the motivation is strong enough to override the forces toward balance—but, being unstable, this state of affairs is not likely to last indefinitely. And so the lessons I have learned are two: that in human affairs any formal, elegant theory is apt to need revision; and that humans, being subject to conflict, ambivalence, ambiguity, and uncertainty, must be understood as they are, not necessarily as the formal theory oversimplifies them.

CONCEPTUAL CONSTANCIES AND OBSERVED INCONSTANCIES

The two anomalies that I have chosen to discuss represent, I suspect, only a tiny sample of those that could be mentioned. (See, for example, Berscheid and Walster, 1969, concerning "exceptions to the reciprocity-of-liking rule" and "limitations to the rule that similarity engenders liking.") But even a much larger sample of empirical deviations from theoretical predictions could, I believe, be subsumed under two general considerations. The first of them is an extension of my earlier assertion that $X \neq X$; it is simply that attraction $\neq$ attraction. Phenomena to which we assign the same label are, to cite Webster's definition of *protean*, "exceedingly variable; readily assuming different shapes or forms." I have elsewhere distinguished, both conceptually and operationally, among several "varieties" of attraction, as associated with forms of "reward value" (positive or negative) attributed to another person (1960). Simple liking (an over-extended term) refers to the rewards stemming from a person's observable characteristics; perceived reciprocity of attraction is another kind of reward; and, third, what I called perceived support, under which I included role support, respect (for another's abilities), and value support (as by attitudinal similarity). My own data (1961) showed some of the conditions under which each of these is prominent.

While such attempts at least point to complexities in the developmental processes of attraction, they represent only a miniscule approach to the task of understanding the complex psychological processes by which attraction is aroused, maintained, and changed. I have come to think of any particular instance of person-to-person attraction as being precarious or vulnerable, in the sense of being subject to constant bombardments that threaten its existing state. It is these potentialities for instability that have recently come to interest me. This is the second of the considerations that seem to me to underlie the anomalies that I have referred to.

And so I turn to questions about the sources of the relative stability of interpersonal attitudes, as compared with nonpersonal ones. They hinge, in the first place, on the fact of interdependence between the attractor and the attractee. If the object of attraction (positive or negative) is seen to change, then the attractee is subject to change—though he may not be aware of his own contribution to the other's change. In any case, his attraction toward the other is literally dependent on the behavior of the other. But, secondly, this dependence is not total; neither the source nor the object of attraction is influenced solely by the other. Each of them is involved in other attraction relationships, which may impinge in various ways upon their relationship with each other—as is known to anyone who has studied the sociometrics of families or other small groups. Abelson's illustration of Joe, Harry, and Ann is a case in point.

Perhaps such considerations seem to present a picture of such instability as to border on indecipherable chaos. As for myself, I find a reasonably firm base in the central notions of balance theory, according to which stability is to be expected not in the dependent variable of attraction—whose vacillations it is our job to account for—but in the property of balance among multiple forces. I have tried to document this point in a paper entitled "Stabilities underlying change in interpersonal attraction" (1963). There I documented the point that, at least in two populations studied over several months, changes in attraction adapted themselves to changes in own or in others' perceived attitudes, or vice versa, according to Heiderian principles (with the important exception that I have discussed as my first anomaly).

Of course I must not leave the implication that "balance is everything"—that it is the one firm ground of stability. As illustrated by my second anomaly, the real world is often such that one simply cannot have, simultaneously, a balanced set of attractions and/or other attitudes, with regard to everything. And so I turn to a more general question: Under what conditions are forces toward interpersonal balance outweighed by other forces?

One might begin with Maslow-like notions of hierarchies of needs— from "physiological" and "safety" to "self-actualization" and "desire to know and understand." His notion, of course, is that, as "lower" needs are met, "at once other (and 'higher') needs emerge and . . . dominate the organism" (1943, p. 375). As a matter of fact, Maslow puts the two of his levels that seem most closely related to interpersonal balance— "love and belonging" and "esteem"— as intermediate, just above "safety" and below "self-actualization." Whether or not Maslow's classification is the best possible one, or whether their ordering is proper—or even, if so, whether any such scheme applies universally to all individuals—these are not my present concern. We know that many individuals are, at least sometimes, subject to the strains of interpersonal imbalance. We also know that needs for balance can be superseded by stronger ones—perhaps habitually, perhaps as situationally determined. We know comparatively little, however, about relative strengths of the different needs, either for people in general, for particular groups, or for particular individuals.

As to personality differences, at least some evidence is available. Following Christie and Cook's finding (1958) that non-authoritarians differentiate attitudes of others more sensitively than do high F-scorers, I analyzed my own data (*The Acquaintance Process*, 1961), and found strong support for this proposition among my 17 subjects. Here is an excerpt from my conclusions:

> The non-authoritarians' characteristic solution to the threat of [imbalance] is nonautistic: they tend to achieve balance not by exaggerating actual agreement with those to whom they are attracted . . . but by judging rather accurately who is in agreement with them, and letting their attractions be determined accordingly. The . . . authoritarians tend to be just the reverse: they tend to perceive more agreement than actually exists with those toward whom they are already attracted (p. 136).

I'm sure that other personality variables, too, affect the position of what Henry Murray might call a need for balance (n *Bal*) in an individual's hierarchy of needs. I got the distinct impression, while poring over my *Acquaintance* data, that some individuals would do almost anything to convince themselves that they were "in balance" with preferred others (at the cost of misjudging the others' attitudes), while some were quite ready to sacrifice balance, their ranks of attraction being quite unrelated to their ranks of perceived agreement. The latter individuals appeared to be generally high in self-esteem and personal security, and some of the former conspicuously low. . . . But these are not confirmed findings; my point is simply that intrapersonal dynamics affect the thresholds of susceptibility to forces toward balance.

Finally, let me revert to an earlier theme. Interpersonal attraction, as between particular individuals, is precarious, in the sense of being vulnerable. It is unstable, in the sense of needing continual reinforcement. It changes over time: witness, for example, the frequency of divorce; and, as another example, the differences between early and late acquaintance. In my own study of the latter phenomena, I found a great deal of volatility during the early weeks of acquaintance, and even in the fourth month change was still occurring—and this in a "controlled" setting. I have long considered it regrettable that a large proportion of empirical data comes from subjects who are known only by verbal description, who have only a slight history of acquaintance with each other or (even worse) whose history of acquaintance is unknown.

From a theoretical viewpoint, variability is of course a prerequisite to the understanding of independent variables. Equally important, I think, is developmental variability in attraction between the same individuals. As researchers, we should exploit this advantage of instability—while at the same time looking for conceptual stabilities that underlie observed vacillations. I know of no theoretical approach that more successfully takes into account *both* the observed instabilities *and* their dependence upon objects and events outside the dyad itself, than that of interpersonal balance theory.

REFERENCES

Abelson, R. P., & Aronson, E., et al (eds.), *Theories of cognitive consistency: A sourcebook.* Chicago: Rand McNally, 1968.

Berscheid, E., & Walster, E. H. (eds), *Interpersonal attraction.* Reading, Massachusetts: Addison-Wesley, 1969.

Christie, R., & Cook, P. A guide to published literature relating to the authoritarian personality through 1956. *Journal of Psychology,* 1956, *45,* 171-199.

Heider, F. Social perception and phenomenal causality. *Psychological Review,* 1944, *51,* 358-374.

Heider, F. Attitudes and cognitive organization. *Journal of Psychology,* 1946, *21,* 107-112.

Heider, F. *The psychology of interpersonal relations.* New York: Wiley, 1958.

Hershkowitz, A. Reported in Jordan, N., Research Paper p-178. Institute for Defense Analysis, Economic and Political Studies Division, Arlington, Virginia, 1966.

Jordan, N. Behavioral forces that are a function of attitudes and of cognitive organization. *Human Relations,* 1953, *6,* 273-287.

Maslow, A. H. A theory of human motivation. *Psychological Review,* 1943, *50,* 370-396.

Morrissette, J. O. An experimental study of the theory of structural balance. *Human Relations,* 1958, *11,* 239-254.

Newcomb, T. M. An approach to the study of communicative acts. *Psychological Review,* 1953, *60,* 393-404.

Newcomb, T. M. *The acquaintance process.* New York: Holt, Rinehart and Winston, 1961.

Newcomb, T. M. Interpersonal balance. In Abelson, R. P., Aronson, E., et al (eds.), *Theories of cognitive consistency*. Chicago: Rand McNally, 1968, pp. 28-51.

Price, K. O., Harburg, E., & Newcomb, T. M. Psychological balance in situations of negative interpersonal attitudes. *Journal of Personality and Social Psychology*, 1966, *3*, 265-270.

Rodrigues, A. The psycho-logic of interpersonal relations. Unpublished doctoral dissertation, University of California, Los Angeles, 1966.

Rodrigues, A. Effects of balance, positivity, and agreement in triadic social relations. *Journal of Personality and Social Psychology*, 1967, *5*, 472-476.

Steiner, I. D., & Spaulding, J. Preference for balanced situations. *Technical report #1*, Grant 4460, United States Public Health Service, University of Illinois, 1966.

Zajonc, R. B., & Burnstein, E. The learning of balanced and unbalanced social structures. *Journal of Personality*, 1965, *33*, 153-163. (a)

Zajonc, R. B., & Burnstein, E. Structural balance, reciprocity, and positivity as sources of cognitive bias. *Journal of Personality*, 1965, *33*, 570-583. (b)

3

Attraction and Power

George C. Homans

In our discussion of interpersonal relations, the word *attraction* is used ambiguously. When we speak of one man's attraction to another, we refer to his liking or admiration for him. We refer to sentiments or attitudes, and they are positive. But we also refer to the man's willingness to approach the other, to be near him, to interact with him. Here we are not talking about attitudes but about overt behavior. And if we assume, as I suspect in the first instance we do, that attitudinal attraction and behavioral attraction are bound to go together, we shall sooner or later find ourselves mistaken. One man may be eager to interact with another without in the least liking him, or, though this is probably rarer, may like him without being eager to interact. A third variable—not the only one but an important one—that may affect the association between the other two is interpersonal power. But power is not really a single variable, for there is more than one kind of power. I shall be talking about the relationship between attitudinal and behavioral attraction as it is conditioned by various forms of power.

What is *power*? The thing is obviously of great weight. But what is it? I once made a casual survey of the definitions given the word. It may refer to physical power, such as the power to pick a man up by the seat of his pants and throw him out the window. But no one would confine the word *power* to physical power. Indeed physical power is only one basis for power of more interesting kinds. Other definitions of the word refer only to one man's capacity to change another's behavior. Consider Herbert Simon's statement (1957, p. 5) : "For the assertion, 'A has power over B', we can substitute the assertion, "A's behavior causes B's behavior." But B's behavior may also cause A's, and we usually think of power as an asymmetrical relationship. Still other definitions try to get out of the difficulty by specifying that one man changes the other's behavior to a greater extent than the other does his, or more often, or over a wider range of activities; or even that the first man can change the behavior of a greater number of other men than the second can. I put all these definitions into a class I call "bare causality." They refer to an event—the change of one man's behavior by the behavior of another— but they are "bare" in the sense of not referring at all to how or why the change takes place.

One man may cause another's behavior by any one of an enormous range of actions: for instance, by kicking a stone in front of his feet so that he stumbles. The next class of definitions specifies more closely the nature of the action each person must take in order that the relationship between them may be considered one of power. The definition refers to the character of the stimulus presented by the first man and the response of the other to it. The first must issue something I shall call generically an *order*—it may be no more than a gesture indicating where he wants the second to go—and the action of the second must correspond with the "order" to some degree. This second class of definition I call "obedience to orders." It is often called authority rather than power. Again Simon (1957, p. 75) writes: "We will say that an individual accepts *authority* when his choice among alternative behaviors is determined by the communicated decision of another." Note that this class of definitions is still "barely causal," since they make no reference to why the second man obeys the orders of the first. And they are neutral with respect to "attraction" in the attitudinal sense. After all, a man may obey another's orders whether or not he is attracted to him.

Only when we get to a class of definitions that begins to ask why one man's behavior changes the behavior of another do we begin to get something that has a direct bearing on attraction. Let us take first the commonest type of definitions of power, from Max Weber's *macht* (1947) onwards. Peter Blau's is a good modern example (1964, p. 117). He says of power that ". . . it is the ability of persons or groups to impose their will on others through deterrence either in the form of withholding regularly supplied rewards or in the form of punishment, inasmuch as the former as well as the latter constitute, in effect, a negative sanction." The classes of definition are not mutually exclusive, and this example certainly falls within that of obedience to orders. But it adds something to mere causality. It suggests a reason why the second man obeys the orders of the first. If he does not obey, the first man is able to apply sanctions—positive punishment or the withholding of rewards. Note that the powerful man is a behaviorist. He believes that actions are what count, and that actions can be made more or less likely by reward or punishment.

But Blau is not quite accurate. It is not actual punishment but the convincing threat of punishment that gives the first man his power. If he punishes the second, it is because the second has disobeyed his orders; that is, his power has failed, not succeeded. It may sound like a paradox, but the more powerful a man is, the less actual punishment he uses. If he punishes from time to time, it is only to make his threats convincing. And if he operates by threat he actually operates through reward and not punishment, since avoidance of punishment is a reward, and compliance with orders accomplishes this.

Power in this sense certainly has implications for attraction, both in the attitudinal and in the behavioral sense. Emotionally, we all assume that in the first instance punishment and its threat release negative emotions—call them anger—in men, and that, therefore, men are apt to dislike persons that may or do punish them. Behaviorally we assume that, since the avoidance of punishment is a reward, men are apt to try to avoid persons that may or do punish them—and avoidance seems to be the opposite of attraction. On second thought, it is not clear that power in this sense always inhibits attraction. It would be one thing if a man had some chance of avoiding a powerful person, but quite another if he could not do so. In the latter case he might be behaviorally drawn toward the powerful, if only to placate him, to anticipate his demands. There is even a question emotionally. So much depends on what a man has come to expect. Suppose a man has come to expect punishment, because he has been punished regularly, or often and at random. Will he still continue to feel anger towards the man who punishes him? In its preoccupation with the positive in human affairs, American social science may not have paid enough attention to questions of this sort.

Finally, suppose he has been punished fairly, that is, whenever he has violated some rule he accepts as right, and never when he has not. Remember that what is right is only expectation at another remove, since what is tends to become what ought to be. Distributive justice is as much concerned with punishment as with rewards, and its attainment can affect emotional reactions to either. I believe that a man is apt to be strongly attracted to another person who punishes him fairly, provided that the punishment enables him to learn to perform actions that ultimately win him highly valued rewards. Just as some of us learn to bite the hand that feeds us, others learn to lick the hand that beats us.

I argue that the determinants of attraction are complex, and that attraction is itself ambiguous. Again American psychology has not adequately studied some of these matters. They involve strong motivations, and strong motivations—passions, if you like—are not easily manipulated in psychological experiments. Indeed, the trouble with many experiments in social psychology is that the subjects do not care very much, one way or the other, what they do in response to experimental manipulation. To understand strong motivation we must, however unscientifically, observe "real life."

But to return to power. Definitions like Blau's are inadequately general even to define power of a particular type. In the first place, they talk about the powerful person's "imposing his will" on the other, and we all know how ambiguous words like "will" are. We shall see that a man may be powerful without imposing anything we can recognize as a "will." Second, they talk about negative sanctions only, and not positive ones as well. Not only social scientists but most of us cannot believe that power is really power unless it works by threats and against resistance. Power is thought to be an evil, though sometimes a necessary one. But how about the man who offers others good money to do a piece of work, and they jump at the chance? Should we not call him powerful? Usually we do not. Finally, these definitions speak only of the sanctions, whether negative or positive, applied by the more powerful to the less, and not about the sanctions, the countervailing power, applied by the less powerful to the more. To understand power in its general meaning we must look at the relation between the two.

Before I offer a more general definition, let me begin with an illustration. The one I always use is taken from Blau's work (1955), but it is easy to find a large number of similar ones in every sphere of human activity. A, an experienced man, and B, an inexperienced one, are employees in an office. At some point each can either stick to his own work or enter into an exchange with the other, such that A gives B help in doing his work and B gives A approval in return. Help is rewarding to B, approval is rewarding to A, but *how* rewarding? If, for each man, the value of the reward to be obtained from the exchange is greater than that to be obtained from the alternative, each of them will, according to a familiar psychological principle, be apt to enter into the exchange. Each has then changed the other's behavior and each, by one of the definitions of the word, has exerted power over the other. But there is still no evidence that one has exerted more power than the other. An asymmetry has yet to be established.   •

Suppose now that a third person, C, inexperienced like B, also wants help and can get it only from A. (Let me point out here that we really cannot consider interpersonal relations in a dyad, without considering possible relations between each member of the dyad and third parties. They always make a difference, except perhaps when two are alone on a desert island.) If A now meets the demands of both B and C, he will have to take more time from his own work, and hence the cost to him of giving help goes up. Since he will be getting approval from two men and not one, the marginal value of this reward tends, by the satiation principle, to go down for him. By both mechanisms A's net reward from giving help in return for approval has declined. As for B, he is in danger of getting less help, since two men are now asking for it where only one did before, and so the net value to him of giving approval in return for help tends to go up. Let us call the perceived net positive reward of each man his *interest*. Then, compared with the initial situation, A's interest in the exchange has fallen compared with B's or C's. An asymmetry is established.

This is the general condition of power of this class. It has been understood for ages by men of affairs. Long ago Waller and Hill (1951, p. 191) called it "the principle of least interest": "That person is able to dictate the conditions of association whose interest in the continuation of the affair is least." The principle is more general than definitions of power such as Blau's, in that it refers not just to the motivations, the interests, of one of the parties but to those of both, and, above all, to the relationship between their interests. It is more general also in that it applies to both positive and negative sanctions. Thus the man who has less to fear from the threats of the other is the more powerful.

But what do we mean when we say that the condition of least interest is a condition of power? Let us go back to the office, where A now has less interest in continuing the exchange than has either B or C. In order to keep help coming from A, in a situation where A's interest in giving help has declined, B is likely to offer in the exchange either more approval or a warmer grade of approval. That is, B has changed his behavior in favor of A while A's behavior has remained the same. Under these circumstances I shall say that A has exerted power over B.

Now for some critical comments. Note, first of all, what has been called the power base: the source of A's power is his monopoly of good advice or, more generally, his command of a scarce capacity to reward, not absolutely scarce but scarce in relation to demand. The monopoly of a scarce good is a common power-base, but not of course the only one. Even the monopoly of the capacity to kill is the monopoly of a scarce good, for the capacity to kill is also the capacity to spare.

Note too that, although power is often defined as a man's capacity to "impose his will" on another, A in our example has not in any obvious sense imposed his will on B or C. Indeed if anyone has a will here, it is the less powerful person: he badly wants help. Nor has A issued anything like an order. Indeed he may be quite unconscious of what is happening. Nor has he threatened to use negative sanctions. To point this out is not in the least to deny that there are situations of power in which wills are imposed, orders issued, and threats made. What it does mean is that these are not essential. All that is essential to power of the present class is a relationship between the net rewards of the two men, such that one has less interest than the other, and an asymmetric change of behavior by the man with the most interest. Since I have not encountered a full and formal definition of power of this class, let me try to state one: when A's net interest, that is, the excess of his rewards over his costs, in taking action that will reward B, is less, at least as perceived by B, than B's net interest in taking action that will reward A, and B as a result changes his behavior in a way favorable to A, then A has exerted power over B.*

From this analysis an important consequence follows: Let us return to our example. Since B's change of behavior increases A's reward from the exchange, and so makes the rewards of the parties more nearly equal again, it has the effect of reducing the power-differential between them. More generally, if the other circumstances surrounding a relationship remain unchanged, the relative power of two persons (or groups) tends towards equality in the course of repeated exchanges. Each person may continue to get the other to do what he, once power has been exerted over him, is now doing, but no more. This is one condition of equilibrium in social relations. There is, of course, no guarantee that the "other circumstances" will remain unchanged or even that the exchanges will be repeated.

Now I want to return to the relationship between power and attraction in either the behavioral or the emotional sense. I have already spoken of the relation between attraction and negative sanctions. I turn now to the relation between it and positive sanctions such as mark the exchange between the experienced and the inexperienced man in the office. In that

---

* For a fuller analysis of this form of power, see G. C. Homans, Fundamental social processes, in N. J. Smelser (ed.), *Sociology: An introduction*. (New York: Wiley, 1967, pp. 51-58).

exchange I had B, the inexperienced man, offering A what I called "approval" in return for the latter's help. In effect, that was all that B had to offer in return, and all that many people can offer in similar circumstances. Ordinarily, approval is not a scarce good; most people are at least "able" to supply it. I want to ask what we mean by words like "approval" and "liking." They are not altogether unambiguous.

Most of us assume that when a man fails to get a reward under circumstances in which he has received one in the past, and in which, therefore, he has come to expect one; or when he has received an unexpected punishment, he will feel and display some degree of an emotion we call anger, and direct it at the perceived source of the punishment or some surrogate. This is, in effect, the frustration-aggression hypothesis. We assume too that this response is to some degree innate and not learned. Do we also assume, by symmetry, that when a man gets a reward under circumstances in which he did not expect one, or fails to receive a punishment when he did, he will feel and display some emotion opposite to anger, and direct it at the perceived source of the reward? Though we should not count on nature to be symmetrical, I believe we do make such an assumption, but we do not make it explicit as we do the frustration-aggression hypothesis, and it is surprising how little research has been done to test it. If we further pursue the symmetry, we must assume that this response, like the response to frustration, is to some degree innate and not learned. I certainly assume that some response of this sort, directed at the person perceived as the source of reward, is one of the things we tap in confidential sociometric tests that ask each member of a group to say which other members he likes or approves of.

But the response in its pure form is not commonly observed. The reason is that approval, like aggression, can also be a learned response, an operant that a man may come to emit more often if it has been rewarded by instrumental success. However much we may spontaneously like a man, we may also learn to express our approval of him, if that action makes more probable his performance of an action that rewards us. Much of the ambiguity of what we mean by attraction lies in the mixture of emotional and instrumental response.

One of the crucial variables in the symmetrical proposition is the degree of expectation. Thus punishment received in expected circumstances is much less likely to arouse anger than punishment in unexpected ones. And therefore reward in unexpected circumstances may be more apt to arouse approval than reward in expected ones. What men expect is determined ultimately by their past experiences, but we must be less interested in the idiosyncratic expectations of particular men than in expectations which, because of their similar past experiences, may be common to many men.

In what follows I am frankly speculating, but let me go ahead and see where I come out. What men generally expect in an exchange between them is something like Aristotle's rule of distributive justice—that if A performs an action that rewards B, then B should perform an action that rewards A. Now in our exchange between the skilled and the unskilled man in the office, the skilled man rewards the unskilled man with help, but the unskilled man rewards the skilled man with what? With approval or, at the extreme, with admiration. It is true that approval may in fact reward the skilled man, but, at least in the first instance, the unskilled man does not look on the matter that way. His behavior has in the first instance some tincture of an unlearned response to his receiving reward when he had no reason to expect it, because he had nothing to offer in return. This I believe is the chief determinant of the emotional attraction of a less powerful man to a powerful one, when power is manifested in a difference in the ability to provide positive rewards. More generally, when the distribution of positive rewards between the two men would otherwise be unbalanced, the reaction of approval by the less powerful man for the more powerful one, the attraction the former feels for the latter, serves to balance the exchange.

There is some evidence that supports this interpretation. If the apparently less powerful man discovers that the powerful one helped him only in order to get something out of him later, so that the exchange was in fact balanced though it did not appear so at the time, then his emotional reaction of approval is destroyed. Indeed the less powerful man has been deceived: he has given more than he should have given in the exchange, and the moral superiority of the powerful man is at an end. It is, above all, moral superiority that attracts admiration.

Again, if the powerful man shows signs of exploiting his power, if, in return for his help, he seems to ask more in the way of the outward signs of admiration from the less powerful one than could fairly be expected, if the less powerful begins to say, "That bastard won't help me unless I crawl"—then too the emotional response of the less powerful man and the moral superiority of the powerful one are at an end. But note here also, in relation to what I said earlier, that the powerful man is no longer making promises but threats, an implied threat of withdrawing help. How close are rewards and punishments to one another! One man gets another hooked on the rewards he has to offer, and then has a hold over him, which he can exploit by threatening to withdraw them. The less powerful man may still go to the powerful one for help, if only because he still needs help and can get it nowhere else. That is, he will be attracted to the other behaviorally, but the attitudinal attraction will be destroyed. One of the things I am most interested in is the relationship between the two kinds of attraction. In a dyad made up of persons of different power, the less powerful will be attracted to the other in both senses, if apart from the attraction, he gets favorable terms, by the standards of distributive justice, in exchange with the other; that is, he gets more than he gives.

I must now introduce another consideration. In his exchanges with B and C in the office, person A establishes the outward and visible signs of his superiority in status to the other two. He provides more of the goods that are scarce—help—and gets more of the goods—approval—that are plentiful. A man's status is his perceived ranking as higher or lower than others on dimensions such as these—perceived not only by himself and by persons in direct exchange with him but also by other members of the group, the audience, who are in a position to observe what is going on. We know that his status in this sense is not often a matter of indifference to a man. Unfortunately, the very act of going to another to ask for help provides the outward sign of one man's inferiority in status to the other. Accordingly, even if the other provides the help on fair terms, a man may be reluctant to go to him often and ask for it. Here something like the reverse of the situation I mentioned earlier may exist; the man may be attracted to another attitudinally but avoid him behaviorally when status is at stake.

But again I must qualify. A man is the more reluctant to go to another in this way the more his present status is similar to that of the other, the more, that is, he stands to lose in comparison with him. If his status is already well established as inferior to that of the other, he will be much less reluctant. Accordingly, if there are actual or potential differences in status between men, the attitudinal attraction of the inferior towards the superior is the more likely to be accompanied by the behavioral attraction the greater the inferiority of the one to the other and the more firmly the inferiority is established. This may explain the attraction some of us feel for great writers, artists, or sports stars. They reward us greatly, but we are so far out of the running in competition with them that they present no threat to us. Unfortunately, though we feel greatly attracted, we have, by the same token, little chance to see our attraction result in personal contact.

I have been talking of the attraction of one man towards another, and have said nothing of mutual attraction. The reason is that I have been concerned with the relation between attraction and power, and power gets in the way of mutual attraction in that the kind of attraction an inferior feels towards a superior can hardly be the same as that which a superior feels towards an inferior. The superior need not have a low opinion of the inferior at all, but the rewards he gets from an inferior are not those the inferior gets from him. Mutual attraction is more likely the more nearly two persons are equal in power and hence in status. This does not of course mean that all persons of equal status are attractive to one another. But if each does find the behavior of the other rewarding, each can be attracted to the other without further considerations getting in the way. And there need be no separation between attitudinal and behavioral attraction. Since they are equal in power, the question of one's exploiting the other, of one's failing to meet the conditions of distributive justice, need not arise. To enjoy one another's behavior they are apt to share similar values, and hence probably similar backgrounds. To be equal in power they are probably similar in behavior in other respects. There is evidence that this mutual attraction is particularly likely to show itself behaviorally in what may broadly be called leisure-time pursuits, and I have elsewhere (Homans, 1961) produced an argument explaining why this should be so.

I have said most of the important things I want to say. But I propose to go on a little longer, in order to make a distinction between power of the last class and power of another sort, though similar to the last in that the definitions are not "barely causal" but make some reference to why the power in question is effective.

In the last class of power, control is what I call *internal to the exchange.* That is, A has the capacity to change B's behavior because A can himself by taking action alter B's outcomes: his rewards and punishments. He may not be able to do so directly, but only because third parties will also obey his orders. Still, it is his action that makes the difference. The present class of power differs from the former in the fact that A need not be able himself to control B's outcomes; control is *external to the exchange.*

Let me take first a simple example. A tells B that if he goes to a certain place he will find good fishing. A has given B an order—though it is not usually looked on as such. He has sent a message to B telling him to do something. B, for any reason you please, does go to the place and finds that the fishing is indeed good. Here A has no means of providing B's reward: he is quite unable to arrange that the fishing will be good at the place he suggested. B's reward comes, if it comes at all, from the external environment, in this case the physical environment. But if

B has been successful, then, by a familiar psychological principle, he is apt to take A's advice again, and by generalization, even to take A's advice about matters other than fishing. Then A has acquired a form of power over B; he is able to control some of B's actions.

If this be power, it is clear that it can display the various kinds of asymmetry. B may take A's advice but not A, B's. A's advice may be taken over a wider range of activities than B's is. Or A may thus be able to control the behavior of a larger number of persons than B can control.

In the example used, I have assumed that A himself was perfectly indifferent whether or not B fished at the place he suggested. In other cases, A may strongly wish B to take a particular action; he himself may be rewarded if B takes the action, but if he cannot personally affect B's reward, his power still falls into this class.

It is true that, once A has established to B's satisfaction the fact that his advice is apt to be good, he has begun to acquire power of the previous class too, for he may then use the threat of withholding advice from B as a means of getting B to do what he wants. Thus in the office situation, I have assumed that A's advice had already been established as good advice. But A cannot in this case acquire power of the previous class without first acquiring power of the present class.

The reverse may also be true; he may not be able to acquire power of the present class without first possessing power of the previous class. Though we may be able to keep the mechanisms analytically separate, powers of the two classes are apt in practice to fuse. On the first occasion—and the first occasion is always critical, since an action not taken is an action that cannot be rewarded—B may be unwilling to accept A's suggestion, and A may have to promise him rewards for doing it or threaten to punish him for not doing it. But if, under this form of power, B does finally take the action and finds that he is rewarded by the external environment, social or physical, then A has begun to acquire power in the present sense too.

This is what happens in the case of successful military leaders. When an officer is new to a unit and bears no reputation other than his rank, he may get his men to obey him through the implication, inherent in his superior rank, that they ought to obey him and will be punished if they do not obey. But once they have obeyed him and found that obedience to him leads to victory over the enemy or at least to the avoidance of casualties perceived to be unnecessary, he will have acquired power in the new sense. After they have experienced a series of successes, they may come, as we say, to follow him blindly. Power in the present sense will have wholly taken over. Vice versa, if obedience does not lead to success against the hostile environment, his followers become more apt to challenge his power in the previous sense.

Into this class falls what is often called "persuasive power." Talcott Parsons (1963, p. 44) writes: "Persuasion is ego's attempt to get compliance by offering reasons why it would, from alter's own point of view, independent of situational advantages, 'be a good thing' for him to act as ego wished." Since it is clear that Parsons means by 'situational advantages' those which ego himself can manipulate, and that the power of persuasion is independent of these, his definition refers to this class of power. But we must remember that, for this form of power to exist, it is not essential that A should "wish" B to behave in any particular way or that A should provide arguments why behaving in that way would be to B's advantage. The bare essentials are that B should at least once and for whatever reason do what A suggests; that B should in fact find the result rewarding, compared with some alternative, and that B's propensity to follow A's suggestion on some new occasion be strengthened accordingly. If my taking a man's advice has in fact brought me unpleasant results, the chances that I shall take his advice the next time have decreased, no matter how cogent in themselves are the arguments he uses. Success, not reason, is the ultimate persuader.

This class of power includes examples more subtle than any I have offered so far. If taking a man's suggestion leads to what is called self-reward, if it leads to the reward that many men experience when they live up to their obligations or meet the demands their ideals put upon them, then he has acquired this kind of power over them. The only condition is that he himself shall not have provided the reward.

Power acquired by showing others how to acquire rewards for themselves would probably, if we were able to measure such things, turn out to be the most important of all forms of power. Men would have a low capacity to get social action from others if they had to rely only on the sanctions they personally were able to control.

Let me turn now to the relation between this class of power and attraction. Since attitudinal attraction is fundamentally determined by positive reward, and since a man acquires this sort of power over another by getting the other rewarded, even though he does not control the reward himself, this power should lead to the less powerful man's being emotionally drawn to the more powerful. Whether he is also behaviorally attracted, in the sense of being eager to interact with the more powerful person, is as usual another question. Let me take only one case. Suppose, as a result of previous experience, that a man perceives obedience to a leader's orders as likely to lead to favorable results for the group of which he is part, and that he, as a member of the group, will participate in this reward. Suppose also that the long-term reward will be obtained only by incurring short-term cost and risks. And suppose finally that others could carry out the task the leader will order as well as the man could himself. Might not the characteristic reaction of a man in this situation be expressed as follows: "I am ready to do what I am asked, but I won't go out of my way to have the leader choose me to do the job rather than someone else?" If this is his reaction, he may well avoid the leader, even though he admires him. His behavioral avoidance will overcome his attitudinal attraction. This is one of the conditions determining the ambivalence men often feel towards persons in power over them, and creating toward such persons an emotional reaction better called respect than whole-hearted liking.

Just to complete the record I want to mention one other thing that people often refer to as power, especially when they talk about "power elites" and the like. So far as the other definitions of power refer to decisions at all, they refer to how and why a decision is carried out in action, and not to the process of reaching the decision itself. The present class of things called power does refer to this latter process; a man has power in his group, organization, or government to the extent that he participates in reaching a decision which is then carried out, through the exercise of other forms of power, by the members of these units. Since a crucial consideration in reaching a decision is precisely whether or not it can or will be carried out in practice, persons who have power in this sense usually have power in the other senses too. This combination is what we refer to when we say that responsibility and authority should go together, that the duty to decide on action should be accompanied by the power to carry out the decision. Accordingly, I shall say nothing more about the relation of attraction to this form of power.

Instead of calling all these analytically separate processes by the name of power, and indeed by other names like influence and authority, it would be to the advantage of social science if we could agree to call each by a separate name. But I despair of reaching any such agreement.

REFERENCES

Blau, P. M. *The dynamics of bureaucracy*. Chicago: University of Chicago Press, 1955, Pp. 99-116.
Blau, P. M. *Exchange and power in social life*. New York: Wiley, 1964, P. 117.
Homans, G. C. *Social behavior*. New York: Harcourt Brace & World, 1961.
Parsons, T. On the concept of influence. *Public Opinion Quarterly*, 1963, *27*, 44.
Simon, H. A. *Models for Man*. New York: Wiley, 1957, P. 5.
Waller, W. W. and Hill, R. *The family*. New York: Dryden Press, 1951, P. 191.
Weber, M. *The theory of social and economic organization*. New York: Oxford University Press, 1947, P. 152.

4

Cognitive and Reinforcement Theories as Complementary Approaches to the Study of Attraction

Donn Byrne and John Lamberth

Partly because dissimilarity is threatening and partly because theory-confrontation has the aura of a grown-up science, it is not unusual to find psychologists pitting one theory against another in an experimentum that never seems to turn out to be the crux. The noncrucial nature of theoretical tests is occasioned by two factors. First, the test of theory X tends to be proposed by the proponents of theory Y. It is much easier to build and be convinced of the solidity of a straw man if it represents the other fellow's position rather than one's own. Second, there are an infinite number of ways to explain or explain away embarrassing data. If worst comes to worst, it is always possible to accommodate the finding by ad hoc modifications of the theory (Kuhn, 1962). Theories are not destroyed in scientific super bowls; rather they gradually lose their popularity. The contribution of empirical data to the rise and demise of theories tends to be cumulative and indirect. This point has been emphasized by Kaplan (1964, p. 152):

The research described in the present paper was supported in part by Research Grant GS-2752 from the National Science Foundation.

The authors wish to thank Herman Mitchell, Don Brown, and Carolyn Hodges for their assistance on this project. Our very special appreciation is given to Mel Lerner and David Novak for their generous help in providing both data and research material.

. . . different interpretations of the experimental findings are always possible; to insist that a particular test is crucial to the correctness of a proposed explanation may very well amount to a begging of the question. Only in fairy tales do Cinderellas have a unique size in footwear, and thieves clap their hands to their heads on hearing the shout that the thief's hat is burning. In sober fact the crucial experiment does not conclusively establish one alternative while making the others absolutely untenable; at most it only alters the balance of probabilities. The issue is always how much trouble we are willing to go to, how much else we are willing to question or to assume, in order to adhere to the chosen alternative.

What is the state of theory and theoretical confrontation in the study of interpersonal attraction?

COGNITIVE AND REINFORCEMENT THEORIES

Much of the research in areas as diverse as animal learning, social psychology, and psycholinguistics can be placed in one of two "opposing" camps: cognitive theory and reinforcement theory. A convincing explanation for the ubiquity of this theoretical schism has been provided by Rychlak (1968). He argues that the dialectical (cognitive) and demonstrative (reinforcement) traditions represent two ends of a dimension of meaning which have been expressed since the writings of the earliest Greek philosophers. Rather than alternative and antagonistic conceptual systems, they may be seen as complementary approaches to the study of behavior and hence of potential mutual benefit.

The Cognitive Approach

Among the characteristics of cognitive theorists is a tendency to approach a research problem subjectively, utilizing introspection and phenomenological analysis. There is often a creative interpretation of the situation, remaining close to one's experience of the "real-life" context in which each new phenomenon may be seen as a special case to be understood. The focus is on the individual and his cognitive processes in which qualitative factors assume primary importance. A few examples of this kind of theorizing by psychologists usually identified with a cognitive orientation may be helpful.

At the lowest level of generality, it is possible to begin with a real world example of a phenomenon, next to induce a mini-hypothesis to account for it, and then to proceed to an experiment designed to test that hypothesis. Aronson (1970, pp. 147-148) typically operates in that fashion:

According to a Gallup poll, John Kennedy's personal popularity increased immediately *after* the Bay of Pigs fiasco. Here is a situation in which a president commits one of history's truly great blunders (up until that time, that is) and, lo and behold, people like him more. Explanation? Perhaps President Kennedy was too perfect. He was young, handsome, bright, witty, a war hero, super wealthy, charming, athletic, a voracious reader, a master political strategist, an uncomplaining endurer of physical pain—with a perfect wife (who spoke several foreign languages), two cute kids (one boy, one girl), and a talented, closeknit extended family. Some evidence of fallibility (like the Bay of Pigs fiasco) could have served to make him human, and hence more likeable.

At a higher level of abstraction, such minihypotheses may form the basis for a broader generalization and a more inclusive conceptual system. Festinger (1954, pp. 118-119) has given us repeated examples of this style:

In many instances, perhaps most, whether or not an opinion is correct cannot be immediately determined by reference to the physical world. Similarly, it is frequently not possible to assess accurately one's ability by reference to the physical world. One could, of course, test the opinion that an object was fragile by hitting it with a hammer, but how is one to test the opinion that a certain political candidate is better than another, or that war is inevitable? Even when there is a possible immediate physical referent for an opinion, it is frequently not likely to be employed. The belief, for example, that tomatoes are poisonous to humans (which was widely held at one time) is unlikely to be tested. The situation is similar with respect to the evaluation of one's abilities. If the only use to which, say, jumping ability was put was to jump across a particular brook, it would be simple to obtain an accurate evaluation of one's ability in this respect. However, the unavailability of the opportunity for such clear testing and the vague and multipurpose use of various abilities generally make such a clear objective test not feasible or not useful ... For both opinions and abilities, to the extent that objective physical bases for evaluation are not available, subjective judgments of correct or incorrect opinion and subjectively accurate assessments of one's ability depend upon how one compares with other persons.

In justifying and explaining the cognitive, person-centered approach, Heider (1958, p. 2) provides an overall rationale which includes the basic assumption that the behavioral sciences are qualitatively different from the physical sciences:

"Intuitive" knowledge may be remarkably penetrating and can go a long way toward the understanding of human behavior, whereas in the physical sciences such common-sense knowledge is relatively primitive. If we erased all knowledge of scientific physics from our world, not only would we not have cars and television sets and atom bombs, we might even find that the ordinary person was unable to cope with the fundamental problems of pulleys and levers. On the other hand, if we removed all knowledge of scientific psychology from our world, problems in interpersonal relations might easily be coped with and solved much as before. Man would still "know" how to avoid doing something asked of him, and how to get someone to agree with him; he would still "know" when someone was angry and when someone was pleased. He could even offer sensible explanations for the "whys" of much of his behavior and feelings. In other words, the ordinary person has a great and profound understanding of himself and of other people which, though unformulated or only vaguely conceived, enables him to interact with others in more or less adaptive ways.

The Reinforcement Approach

The reinforcement approach, in contrast, includes a tendency to attack a research problem objectively by utilizing extraspection and an analysis of situational factors. Variables are seen as relevant to more abstract principles so that a given phenomenon represents simply an example of a more general case. The focus tends to be on stimulus variables and their effects on behavior; the relationship between stimuli and responses is expressed quantitatively whenever possible. The starting point for a given piece of research is less likely to be an anecdote or cocktail party observation; instead, a general theoretical model is the source of deduced hypotheses. Again, a few examples may be helpful.

One strategy is to take a general model such as the classical conditioning interpretation of attraction and deduce a series of hypotheses, as exemplified by Griffitt and Guay (1969, p. 2):

A unique feature of the reinforcement model is the lack of a requirement that the stimulus object to be evaluated have a functional relationship to reinforcing stimuli. That is, a stimulus object need only be present and discriminable at the time of positive or negative reinforcement to assume positive or negative meaning to the responder. The stimulus object may be *any* previously neutral object (human or nonhuman) and may be either directly responsible for or not responsible for but only associated in time with, reinforcing stimuli.

A related strategy is to take an explicit theoretical function and derive its implications for specific instances. Clore and Baldridge (1970, p. 178) follow this approach in explaining why differentially important issues would not be expected to have differential effects on attraction in the typical research design:

Byrne and Rhamey proposed a simple mathematical model which expresses the manner in which differently weighted information should combine to influence attraction. According to a slightly revised version of the model,

$$A_x = m \left(\frac{\Sigma (PR . M)}{\Sigma (PR . M) + \Sigma (NR . M')} \right) + k,$$

or attraction toward a person, X, is a positive linear function of the sum of the *weighted* positive information divided by the sum of the *weighted* positive information plus the sum of the *weighted* negative information. An important prediction of this model, which accounts for the previous negative findings, is that when the positive and negative information (or agreements and disagreements) are equally weighted $(M = M')$, the item weights cancel out and the importance of the issue ceases to affect attraction.

It is sometimes possible to take a formulation such as Hull-Spence behavior theory, supporting data from a vastly different context (different stimuli, different responses, and different species), and utilize these to make quite specific predictions concerning a phenomenon not originally conceptualized within the theory. This procedure is typically followed by the Lotts and their associates (e.g., Lott, Aponte, Lott, & McGinley, 1969, p. 102):

The purpose of the present experiment is to demonstrate that a more positive attitude, or greater attraction, will develop toward a stimulus person who is consistently associated with immediate reward than toward one who is consistently associated with delayed reward.

The hypothesis of the present study follows from Hull's proposal that "the greater the delay in reinforcement, the weaker the secondary reinforcement . . ." (1952, p. 128), and from rat studies by Jenkins (1950) and Logan (1952) which report data that provide support for this proposition.

Reconciling the Two Theoretical Styles

It is tempting, and one of the most predictable of human responses, to identify oneself with one of these two approaches and to point out the wit and wisdom of that approach in comparison to the obviously unexciting and dimwitted weaknesses of the other approach. Thus, we have all witnessed exchanges between the loose thinkers and the nitpickers, the mystics and those hung up with meaningless rigor, the artists and the engineers, those who anthropomorphize and those who reduce the human being to a machine, the soft-headed and the hard-nosed, the armchair thinkers and the gadgeteers, and so on.

One difficulty with forming two hostile armies is that many of us turn out to have both uniforms in the closet. For example, Byrne and Clore may easily be identified as soft-headed cognitive psychologists (1967) or as hard-nosed reinforcement theorists (1970). What if we take an entirely different tack? What if we attempt to view theoretical differences not in terms of the good guys versus the bad guys or the Bull Dogs versus the Red Devils but as useful alternatives to the same goal? Rychlak (1968, p. 457) suggests the utility of this view:

> This historical bifurcation speaks out to proclaim that meanings, facts, ideas, hunches, and so on, vacillate between the poles of doubt and certainty, denotative clarity and connotative implication, creative error and creative accuracy, and so on. These are different ways of expressing the same thing—i.e., that knowledge grows as meanings change and as evidence is brought to bear. Our dimension is unresolvable because in its essentials it describes what *must take place* for meaning to advance. Its import is that it charges each of us with the responsibility of not overlooking his left hand while he turns the knobs of science with his right. A complete explication of our data cannot be found *only* in one end of this dimension of

meaning. We must avoid thinking in terms of only one side, and cross over whenever and wherever it is possible to do so. The more crossings the better, for such journeys to the other side will serve to educate us and raise our level of meaningful understanding.

Our intention here is to provide an example of an attempt to cross from one dimension to the other within attraction research.

PREDICTING ATTRACTION IN A NOVEL SITUATION

From the viewpoint of a reinforcement model of attraction (Byrne, 1969, in press, Byrne & Clore, 1970), the prediction of attraction responses is a matter of applying general theoretical principles to the specifics of a given situation. A major tenet of the general theory has been noted above in the Byrne-Rhamey formula. In a wide variety of instances, the slope and Y-intercept empirically established by Byrne and Nelson (1965) are found to be of predictive utility; the formula is $Y = 5.44X + 6.62$ in which Y is attraction as measured by a specific scale, and X is the weighted proportion of positive reinforcements as defined by the Byrne-Rhamey formula.

One of the more utilitarian features of any general theoretical statement is that a large number of diverse specific elements may be reduced to a small number of theoretical constructs. For example, in attraction research, positive reinforcements have included similar attitudes, positive personal evaluations, physically attractive facial features, bonus points, high performance ratings, a mirth-inducing movie, and similar responses to various personality tests, while negative reinforcements have included dissimilar attitudes, negative personal evaluations, physically unattractive facial features, uncomfortable temperature and humidity conditions, low performance ratings, an overcrowded room, a depression-inducing movie, and dissimilar responses to various personality tests (Byrne, 1961; Byrne, & Griffitt, 1969; Byrne, Griffitt, & Stefaniak, 1967; Byrne, London, & Reeves, 1968; Byrne & Rhamey, 1965; Gouaux, 1970a; Griffitt, 1966, 1968, 1970; Griffitt & Guay, 1969).* If the goal of science is conceptual-

---

* For those who still have concerns about the circularity of reinforcement principles, it is pointed out that stimuli which affect attraction are found to exhibit reinforcement properties in a variety of learning situations (e.g., Byrne, Griffitt, & Clore, 1968; Byrne, Young, & Griffitt, 1966; Clore, 1966; Golightly & Byrne, 1964; Gouaux, 1970b; Lamberth, 1970; Lamberth & Craig, in press; Lamberth & Gay, 1969; Reitz, Douey, & Mason, 1968). Reinforcement is thus defined in terms of specific transituational effects.

ized as the prediction of a maximal number of phenomena from a minimal number of principles, clearly the attraction formula is a step toward a science of attraction.

One point is sometimes a source of confusion. General principles may be applied to any situation in which the relevant stimulus and response components are known. For example, if a stimulus is known to have specific reinforcing properties, learning principles allow us to predict the effects of that stimulus on an instrumental response, and the principles of attraction theory allow us to predict the effects of that stimulus on the evaluation of associated stimuli. One view of the task of behavioral science is the formulation of such principles and the identification of such properties. What if one decides to investigate the effects of a new stimulus? According to Aronson (1970), it is here that reinforcement theory proves to be of little use with respect to prediction. It may come as a suprise, but all formal theories are useless in the sense that Aronson means. No science can predict in the absence of information about the properties of the independent and dependent variables— necromancy can perhaps, but not science.

If we assume that the law of attraction may have some utility, and if we wish to apply it in a novel situation, two alternatives are open. First, we may utilize various procedures to determine the relevant properties of the new variable. Thus, it is a prerequisite that we *measure* mass or temperature or brightness or whatever *before* the general principles are of any predictive value in the situation. Second, we may approach the novel situation subjectively and attempt to predict via experience and empathy what the effects might be. Both approaches are reasonable, and both are legitimate procedures in a young science with a dearth of measuring devices. In the context of a specific research problem, we will suggest the advantages of maintaining a tolerance for and even an espousal of both procedures.

THE EFFECTS OF SIMILARITY AND DISSIMILARITY WHEN THE OTHER PERSON IS EMOTIONALLY DISTURBED

Though the law of attraction is frequently misrepresented (e.g., Senn, 1970; Taylor, 1970) as dealing with similarity, it does in fact deal with the effect of reinforcement on attraction. The effect of similarity on attraction is a special case of the more general law and is not assumed to result from any unique qualities inherent in similarity. Instead, similarity is rewarding and dissimilarity punishing because of the *meaning* of such stimulus qualities to most individuals in a wide variety of situations. In the majority of experiments in the attraction paradigm, the stranger has been presented as a member of the subject's peer group. When we turn to the effects on attraction of similarity to individuals outside of the peer group, the meaning of similarity might well be expected to change, thus altering its reinforcement properties. As a demonstration of that kind of truism with evaluational stimuli, we once arranged a situation in which subjects were found to like a stranger who gives them a negative evaluation and dislike a stranger who gives them a positive evaluation (Mueller, 1969).* Taylor (1970, p. 108) has inaccurately asserted (in italics even) that *"The Byrne research tends to ignore the conditional variables that might completely reverse the similarity-attraction relationship or cancel it altogether."* Beginning with the initial studies in the paradigm (Byrne, 1961a, 1961b, 1962), it has been precisely such "conditional variables" that have been a major focus of interest. One test of the viability of our particular reinforcement model would be its ability to account for and predict anomolies in the similarity-attraction relationship. We will examine a cognitively-oriented and a reinforcement-oriented analysis of changes in the similarity effect when the stranger is not a peer.

Novak and Lerner (1968) proposed a motive which could operate to make similarity unpleasant or even threatening: the need to believe that there is an appropriate fit between our behavior and what fate deals out in rewards and punishments.

> If people were not able to believe they could get what they want and avoid what they dislike by performing certain appropriate acts, they would be anxious, and, in the extreme, incapacitated. Because of the importance of this belief, the person is continually vulnerable to objective evidence that fate can be capricious and beyond one's efforts. This vulnerability becomes important in situations where the person is confronted with someone who has been seriously harmed through no apparent fault of his own—for example, someone with a severe physical or emotional handicap. The presence of such a person may elicit the threatening thought, "Can this also happen to me?" The person would prefer to believe that such a terrible fate can occur only to someone who has deserved it by virtue of having

---

* The secret was that the subjects had communicated to the stranger attitudes which were the opposite of their true beliefs. Obviously, a positive evaluation elicits a positive response in most instances (e.g., Byrne & Griffitt, 1966; Byrne & Rhamey, 1965), but not if the situational context has reversed its meaning.

committed some undesirable act . . . or because of an inherent personal failing . . . in any case, someone unlike himself (Novak & Lerner, 1968, pp. 147-148).

Selecting emotional disturbance as the unpleasant handicap, they proposed that similarity to a disturbed other should be negatively reinforcing and dissimilarity positively reinforcing. In other words their analysis provides a way of guessing at the reinforcement value of specific stimuli before the fact.

The subjects were Kentucky undergraduates. They reported to the experiment in same-sex pairs, and, in separate rooms, they were asked to fill out an attitude questionnaire. Afterward, these questionnaires were supposedly exchanged, but each subject actually received material prepared by the experimenter. In the similar condition, 20 of the 26 attitude items were prepared as similar to those of the subject or as dissimilar. On a 10-item experiences and aspirations questionnaire, similarity and dissimilarity were also manipulated. In addition, each subject received a personal data sheet with such background information as age, year in school, etc., plus an "other information" question which was either filled out "None" or with a paragraph indicating that the person had had a nervous breakdown leading to hospitalization the previous fall, was presently seeing a psychiatrist, and was feeling "shaky" at the moment.

The dependent variable included a measure of attraction which has become standard within the present paradigm, the Interpersonal Judgment Scale (IJS). This instrument consists of six seven-point rating scales dealing with evaluations of the other person's intelligence, knowledge of current events, morality, and adjustment. The last two items, liking and desirability as a work partner, are summed to yield the attraction measure which ranges from 2 to 14 and has a split-half reliability of .85 (Byrne & Nelson, 1965).

The mean attraction responses are shown in Table 1.* It is clear that the usual similarity effects were found with the normal stranger and that they are modified when the stranger is described as emotionally disturbed. There is still a preference for the similar stranger, but the attraction response is less positive than in the parallel normal condition; there is also a slightly less negative rating of the dissimilar disturbed stranger.

---

* It should be noted that Novak and Lerner were particularly interested in whether the subject would choose to approach or avoid the partner. Here, their predicted reversal was obtained in that subjects tend to want to avoid the dissimilar normal partner and the similar disturbed partner.

An additional finding was reported with respect to the adjustment item of the IJS. For this variable, the disturbed partner was seen as less well adjusted, and similarity also exerted a significant effect. Therefore, the partners who were seen as best adjusted were the normals who were similar to the subject. The most maladjusted were those who were dissimilar and disturbed. It may be seen that the manipulation of the stranger's state of adjustment was successful, and this manipulation resulted in a mitigation of the similarity effect.

TABLE 1. *Mean Attraction Responses toward Similar and Dissimilar Strangers Identified as Normal or Emotionally Disturbed*

	Dissimilar	Similar
Normal	7.50	11.04
Emotionally disturbed	8.20	9.67
	(Novak & Lerner, personal communication)	

Conceptualizing the Mitigating Effect in Different Ways

Now we come to a crucial question with respect to this or any other empirical finding. What are the implications of the data? At the simplest and least abstract level, it could be said that the emotional adjustment of the stranger (as operationally defined) constitutes a boundary condition within which the similarity-attraction function is altered. It has been said, with varying degrees of comprehension, that such a finding limits the generality of the similarity effect. Analogously, altitude "limits the generality" of the relationship between temperature and the boiling point. In any event, it would be possible empirically to establish an infinite number of specific instances in which the attraction formula would necessarily be altered in order to predict accurately in each new situation. Further, each new finding could be interpreted in a cognitive fashion with respect to the meaning of the stimulus situation from the subject's point of view, using commonsense examples, anecdote, and analogy.

At the same time, it is equally reasonable to attempt to reduce the variables to more basic and less qualitative abstractions in order to increase the generality of our descriptions. It is here that the formal theoretical framework is of critical importance in increasing both the scope and the precision of our predictions. If one assumes that attraction is a simple linear function of positive and negative stimulus elements, any attraction effect can be explained by analyzing the stimulus context in those terms. The obvious parallels between this approach and that of Anderson's (1968) information processing model should be noted.

In the Novak and Lerner experiment, the two normal stranger conditions should clearly be like the usual conditions in our attraction experiments. Attraction toward a stranger is found to be a linear function of proportion of similar attitudes whether the attitudes are expressed in paper and pencil form (Byrne, 1961), on a tape recording or in a movie (Byrne & Clore, 1966), in a face-to-face interaction with a stooge (Byrne & Griffitt, 1966), or in a face-to-face interaction between two individuals expressing their genuine attitudes (Brewer & Brewer, 1968; Byrne, Ervin, & Lamberth, 1970). A different problem is posed by the emotionally disturbed conditions of Novak and Lerner. If the model is correct, information that the stranger is emotionally disturbed must involve additional elements in the stimulus complex. A general positive effect of a new stimulus (e.g., Griffitt, 1968) or a general negative effect (e.g., Griffitt, 1970) can be readily explained in terms of an increase in the number and/or magnitude of the positive or negative reinforcements associated with X. An interactive effect is slightly more complicated. Palmer (1969) was the first to deal successfully with an interactive effect. With respect to his finding of an interaction between attitude similarity and information about the competence of a stranger, he simply assumed that a stranger's competence embodies both positive and negative qualities for the subject. The way in which this accounts for an interaction will become clear shortly.

Following Palmer's example, we will assume that emotional disturbance in others has both positive and negative stimulus qualities and hence elicits both positive and negative affect. Besides the mathematical necessity for this assumption, the same idea can be justified in cognitively oriented commonsense terms. An emotionally disturbed person in our culture is interesting, pitiable, and amusing; at the same time he is frightening, disgusting, and upsetting. Both aspects of our attitudes about mental illness are frequently depicted on television and in movies. With respect to the attitudinal material, no special assumptions are required. All of the Novak and Lerner subjects received 26 units of attitudinal information (20+ and 6− or the reverse) and 10 units of questionnaire information (8+ and 2− or the reverse). In addition, those receiving the emotionally disturbed paragraph were exposed to an unknown quantity of positive and negative affective stimulation. By working backwards from a curve-fitting process in one of the cells (disturbed-similar), it was found that the assignment of the tentative values of 11+, 22− to the stimulus resulted in the obtained mean matching that predicted by the Byrne-Nelson formula. That is, finding that the stranger had had a nervous breakdown, had been hospitalized, was seeing a psychiatrist, and was feeling shaky was equivalent to having him agree with the subject on eleven topics *and* disagree on 22 topics. With respect to all three stimulus elements, the resulting values to be inserted in the attraction formula are shown in Table 2.

TABLE 2. *Units of Positive and Negative Reinforcement in the Novak and Lerner Experiment*

Emotional Condition	Attitudes			
	Dissimilar		Similar	
Normal	+	−	+	−
Attitude Scale	6	20	20	6
Experiences-Aspirations	2	8	8	2
Other information	0	0	0	0
Proportion of Positive				
Reinforcements		.22	.78	
Disturbed				
Attitude Scale	6	20	20	6
Experiences-Aspirations	2	8	8	2
Other information	11	22	11	22
Proportion of Positive				
Reinforcements		.28	.57	

The quantities presented in Table 2 were then used to determine the weighted proportion of positive reinforcements received by subjects in each condition of the experiment. The resulting values were substituted in the attraction formula ($Y = 5.44X + 6.62$), and the outcome may be seen in Table 3. The close correspondence between the predicted and obtained values is apparent but is the occasion for only muted celebration. The two normal conditions simply indicate that an attraction formula derived in a sample of Texas undergraduates is an accurate predictor of the responses of a sample of Kentucky undergraduates. The new reinforcement values were derived in the disturbed-similar condition, so the nearly identical values for predicted and observed means are obviously only a testament to our arithmetic skills and not a coup de theorie. The sole test of the post hoc values is provided via cross-validation in the disturbed-dissimilar condition in which values derived in a

TABLE 3.   *Predicted and Obtained Attraction Responses in the Novak
and Lerner Experiment*

Condition	Weighted Proportion of Positive Reinforcements	Predicted Attraction Response	Obtained Attraction Response
Normal-Similar	.78	10.86	11.04
Disturbed-Similar	.57	9.72	9.67
Disturbed-Dissimilar	.28	8.14	8.20
Normal-Dissimilar	.22	7.82	7.50

different condition clearly lead to an accurate prediction of the attraction response.

This little exercise has shown, then, that the Novak and Lerner data can be conceptualized in more than one way, which is no news. More importantly, it suggests the strength of the reinforcement approach in reducing varied and complex stimuli to a few basic constructs which have transituational generality and which may be treated in simple mathematical equations. It would be of much greater importance if it were possible to utilize these concepts to make novel predictions in a different situation. If the following research were interpreted as a test of competing theories, it could best be described by borrowing the words of Underwood and Keppel (1967, p. 191):

> It is simple to pose the empirical question, but to get an unambiguous answer empirically is not so simple. At a philosophical level we tend to eschew the crucial experiment for the simple reason that they rarely turn out to be crucial. However, our philosophy was not quite strong enough to prevent our trying the two experiments which will be reported now.

Eliminating and Duplicating the "Emotionally Disturbed" Effect

If the general model is correct, it follows that the appropriate manipulations of the number and/or strengths of the positive and negative reinforcers present in the situation could result in the nullification of the effect of the stranger's emotional disturbance or in the creation of that same "mitigating" effect by quite different stimuli. The predictions which are made at this point depend entirely on the attributes of the theoretical model and on reinforcement value established in previous research.*

Eliminating the "Emotionally Disturbed" Effect

If information about another person's emotional disturbance has a quantitative rather than a qualitative effect on attraction, it may be seen that the addition of other quantities to the stimulus complex could serve to alter that effect in any desired manner. Our strategy was to

* In the two experiments to be described, half of the conditions in each instance constituted attempts at exact replication of those reported by Novak and Lerner. The mean attraction responses toward similar and dissimilar normal and disturbed strangers are given in Tables 5 and 6. Their basic finding with the attraction response was replicated in that the relationship between attitude similarity and attraction is greater in the normal condition ($r_b = .93$) than in the disturbed condition ($r_b = .47$). In addition, it was found that the similar stranger is rated as more intelligent than the dissimilar one ($F = 8.82$, df $= 1/36$, $p < .01$) and the normal stranger as more intelligent than the disturbed one ($F = 6.86$, df $= 1/36$, $p < .02$). The adjustment ratings were also influenced by both independent variables (similarity versus dissimilarity: $F = 7.82$, df $= 1/36$, $p < .01$; normal versus disturbed: $F = 6.52$, df $= 1/36$, $p < .02$). On the Novak and Lerner response measures, similarity affected the adjective measure of attraction ($F = 20.53$, df $= 1/36$, $p < .001$) and the perception of similarity ($F = 15.62$, df $= 1/36$, $p < .001$). In addition, the normal stranger was rated more positively on the adjectives than was the disturbed stranger ($F = 15.44$, df $= 1/36$, $p < .001$). Their findings with the avoidance index were not replicated in that the Purdue subjects did not indicate a desire to avoid anyone, regardless of similarity or emotional state.

There is another incidental finding of note. Our desire was to replicate the Novak and Lerner procedures as closely as possible. In the emotionally disturbed condition, they had the experimenter give the impression of having left the personal data sheet inadvertently. The experimenter pretended to notice it and then removed it with apparent surprise after giving the subject time to read it. With our first groups of subjects at Purdue, we omitted the removal procedure because we felt that the information alone should have the effect. To our surprise, the mean attraction responses toward the dissimilar (9.10) and similar (11.22) disturbed strangers were as high as those toward the equivalent normal strangers (8.10 and 11.90). We almost gave the project up, concluding that the Novak and Lerner findings were not replicable or that we were inept. On a hunch, the disturbed groups were rerun with new groups of subjects with the inclusion of the little dramatization of removing the personal data sheet. That alteration in procedure not only yielded the appropriate results but a disturbed stranger whose data sheet is undisturbed is liked better than one whose personal data sheet is taken away in mid-experiment ($F = 3.81$, df $= 1/35$, $p =$ approximately .05). This difference was even greater on the adjective measure of attraction ($F = 7.42$, df $= 1/35$, $p < .01$). This unintentional finding suggests the extreme sensitivity of our measures to rather small variations in the experimental situation. It also suggests that written information about emotional disturbance is not an effective stimulus. Further research is needed to determine whether the experimenter's removal of the sheet simply focuses attention on that information and makes it more salient or whether removal makes the information appear more socially undesirable or whatever.

replicate the Novak and Lerner normal conditions and then to recreate their disturbed conditions with one change. That change was the addition of a sufficient number of attitudes attributed to the stranger to make the proportion of positive reinforcements approximately equal in the normal and disturbed conditions. In Table 4 it may be seen how this

TABLE 4. *Eliminating the Emotionally Disturbed Effect*

| Emotional | Attitudes | | | |
Condition	Dissimilar		Similar	
Normal	+	−	+	−
Attitude Scale	6	20	20	6
Experiences-Aspirations	2	8	8	2
Other Information	0	0	0	0
Proportion of Positive				
Reinforcements	.22		.78	
Disturbed				
Attitude Scale	4	52	52	4
Experiences-Aspirations	2	8	8	2
Other Information	11	22	11	22
Proportion of Positive				
Reinforcements	.17		.72	

goal was accomplished. The hypotheses are clear-cut. If emotional disturbance represents a special condition which necessarily mitigates the similarity-attraction effect, an interaction will be found. If emotional disturbance represents an established set of specific positive and negative elements (e.g., 11+, 22−), there will be only a main effect for attitude similarity which is actually a main effect for proportion of positive reinforcements.

The experiment was conducted using 38 Purdue undergraduates (16 males, 22 females) as subjects, and the Novak and Lerner procedures were employed. The only alteration was the use of a 56-item attitude scale in the disturbed condition rather than a 26-item scale.

The results are shown in Table 5. Analysis of variance indicates a significant effect only for the similarity variable ($F = 29.86$, $df = 1/34$, $p < .0001$) as predicted by the reinforcement model. The interaction yields an F-ratio less than one.

TABLE 5. *Mean Attraction Responses toward Similar and Dissimilar Strangers Identified as Normal or Emotionally Disturbed in First Byrne and Lamberth Experiment*

Emotional Condition	Attitudes Dissimilar	Similar	Total
Normal	8.10	11.90	10.00
Disturbed	7.89	10.67	9.28
(+ 56 attitudes)			
Total	7.99	11.28	

Duplicating the "Emotionally Disturbed" Effect

The second experiment approached the same theoretical issue from the opposite direction. If the information about another person's emotional disturbance has a quantitative rather than a qualitative effect on attraction, that same effect should be attainable by the addition of the appropriate number of positive and negative elements to the stimulus complex—even though the added elements have no relationship to emotional disturbance. The strategy here was to replicate the Novak and Lerner disturbed condition and then to recreate their normal condition with one change. That change is the addition of other positive and negative reinforcements approximately equal to the 11 +, 22 −value attributed to emotional disturbance. The new material consisted of personal evaluations of the subject by the stranger, an item of information which has been repeatedly established as having a weight of three (Byrne & Ervin, 1969; Byrne & Griffitt, 1966; Byrne & Rhamey, 1965). That is, one positive personal evaluation is equivalent to three similar attitudes, and one negative personal evaluation is equivalent to three dissimilar attitudes. Therefore, if a stranger expressed four positive evaluations of the subject (4 × 3 = 12) and seven negative evaluations (7 × 3 = 21) the resulting reinforcements theoretically approximate those attributed to emotional disturbance. Table 6 indicates how the conditions were created. Again the hypotheses are straightforward. If emotional disturbance represents a special condition which necessarily mitigates the similarity-attraction effect, an interaction will be found. If emotional disturbance represents an established set of specific positive and negative elements (11+, 22−), the evaluative information will have approximately the same effect (12+, 21−) and there will be only a main effect

TABLE 6.   *Duplicating the Emotionally Disturbed Effect*

Emotional Condition	Attitudes			
	Dissimilar		Similar	
Normal	+	−	+	−
Attitude Scale	6	20	20	6
Experiences-Aspirations	2	8	8	2
Other Information	0	0	0	0
Evaluations	12	21	12	21
Proportion of Positive Reinforcement	.29		.58	
Disturbed				
Attitude Scale	6	20	20	6
Experiences-Aspirations	2	8	8	2
Other Information	11	22	11	22
Proportion of Positive Reinforcement	.28		.57	

for similarity. Again, that main effect is actually the proportion of positive reinforcements.

The second experiment used 40 Purdue undergraduates (24 males, 16 females) as subjects and again employed the Novak and Lerner procedures. In the evaluation conditions, the Byrne-Rhamey (1965) methodology was utilized in which the subject is given feedback concerning the stranger's evaluation of him. In this instance, each subject received four positive and seven negative evaluations on a special 11-item IJS. Beyond the original six IJS scales, the ratings dealt with the subject's desirability as a roommate, physical attractiveness, interestingness, open-mindedness, and whether he would make one feel at ease.

The results are shown in Table 7. Once again, as predicted by the reinforcement model, there is a highly significant main effect for similarity ($F = 12.32$, df $= 1/36$, $p < .002$) while the interaction yields an F-ratio less than one.

The objection might be raised that mixed evaluations could be interpreted by the subject as indicative of emotional disturbance, pushing us back to a qualitative rather than a quantitative interpretation of the results. The evidence does not support this notion. On the adjustment item of the IJS, the stranger with mixed evaluations was rated as better adjusted (4.70) than was the emotionally disturbed stranger (3.60) ($F = 6.96$, df $= 1/36$, $p < .01$). Even though the two kinds of information

TABLE 7. *Mean Attraction Responses toward Similar and Dissimilar Strangers Identified as Normal or Emotionally Disturbed in Second Byrne and Lamberth Experiment*

Emotional	Attitudes		
Condition	Dissimilar	Similar	Total
Normal	7.20	9.70	8.45
(+ Evaluations)			
Disturbed	7.80	9.70	8.75
Total	7.50	9.70	

had identical effects on attraction, they were quite distinguishable with respect to adjustment.

Further Predictions from the Model

In the experiments just described, the reinforcement model of attraction was pitted against informal speculations about the effects of the stranger's emotional state on attraction toward him. The specificity of the model made it possible to construct experimental situations in which predictions could be made in the familiar form: if X, then Y.

In this particular instance, there are two problems to be considered with respect to our predictions. First, the model's accuracy was confirmed in part by nonsignificant effects. That is, if the hypotheses were correct, the row and interaction effects would not be significant. They did not reach acceptable levels of significance, but the null hypothesis is a somewhat dubious theoretical base. Second, even where differences were predicted (as with the column effects), a weakness common to most psychological research may be seen. Both Meehl (1967) and Lykken (1968) have pointed out problems with theoretical predictions of differences when point-values are not specified. The better the experiment, the greater the likelihood of finding significant differences and thus "supporting the theory." Meehl (1967, p. 111) notes:

> I conclude that the effect of increased precision, whether achieved by improved instrumentation and control, greater sensitivity in the logical structure of the experiment, or increasing the number of observations, is to yield a probability approaching ½ of corroborating our substantive theory by a significance test, *even if the theory is totally without merit.*

The contracting state of affairs in a field such as physics is one in which at least the *form* of a function is predicted or more commonly a quantitative magnitude or point-value. The result is that ". . . in physics the effect of improving precision or power is that of *decreasing* the prior probability of a successful experimental outcome if the theory lacks verisimilitude, that is, precisely the reverse of the situation obtaining in the social sciences" (Meehl, 1967, p. 113).

Among other possibilities, the solution would seem to be to develop theories which do generate point-predictions or predictions of the form of the function. It may be noted that the present reinforcement model generates both types of predictions. That is, the formula allows us to predict that the responses of the subjects in the eight conditions of the two experiments should yield a linear function; further, the specific mean responses of each condition are predicted. The eight conditions and the predictions concerning them are summarized in Table 8.

TABLE 8. *Predicted and Obtained Attraction Responses in the Byrne and Lamberth Experiments*

Condition	Weighted Proportion of Positive Reinforcements	Predicted Attraction Response	Obtained Attraction Response
Normal-Similar	.78	10.86	11.90
Disturbed-Dissimilar (+ 56 Attitudes)	.72	10.54	10.67
Normal-Similar (+ Evaluations)	.58	9.78	9.70
Disturbed-Similar	.57	9.72	9.70
Normal-Dissimilar (+ Evaluations)	.29	8.20	7.20
Disturbed-Dissimilar	.28	8.14	7.80
Normal-Dissimilar	.22	7.82	8.10
Disturbed-Dissimilar (+ 56 Attitudes)	.17	7.54	7.89

First, trend analysis indicates that the overall linear trend is significant ($F = 44.44$, df $= 1/64$, $p < .001$) while the nonlinear component is not ($F = .58$, df $= 6/64$, n.s.).* Thus, the hypothesis concerning the function was confirmed. The relationship is depicted graphically in Figure 1.

* Through random elimination of subjects, cell frequencies were equalized ($N = 9$) for the trend analysis.

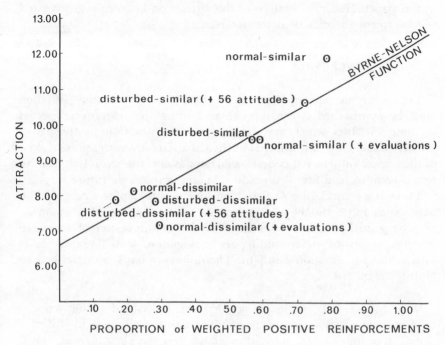

FIG. 1. *Attraction as a linear function of proportion of weighted positive reinforcements.*

Second, Grant's (1962) technique was used to test the fit between the predicted and obtained responses. Two F-ratios were computed. The F for deviations from the model was nonsignificant (F = .11, df = 2/72, $p < .001$). The F for correspondence between the model and the data was highly significant (F = 5.39, df = 6/72, $p < .001$). These analyses indicate not only a lack of significant departure from the predicted values but also a significant positive relationship between that which was predicted and the responses actually obtained. The overall performance of the model is one of remarkable accuracy.

Let it be emphasized that these various analyses of the data are not intended and should not be interpreted as demonstrations of the superiority of a reinforcement theory over a cognitive theory. Rather, they show the utility of a formal quantitative theory over an informal qualitative one—a difference with which few are likely to quarrel. When cognitive theories are developed in an equivalent manner (e.g., Abelson & Rosenberg, 1958; Cartwright & Harary, 1956; Newcomb, 1968), the final structure no longer fits the description of cognitive theories given earlier in this paper. Hence, at that point the distinction between cognitive and reinforcement theories becomes irrelevant.

CONCLUSION

The point has already been made that a novel stimulus situation must be approached either through measuring the relevant properties of those variables which are operating in the situation or through a subjective and empathic analysis of the situation. Given the present state of the science in personality and social psychology, the second alternative would seem to be a useful procedure for the foreseeable future.

There is a second aspect of the cognitive versus reinforcement dichotomy which must also be considered. An understanding of phenomena may be gained at both extremes of Rychlak's dimension of meaning. The two aspects of understanding are analogues of what therapists label intellectual and emotional insight. The difference has been described by Holt (1962, p. 388) :

> In one sense, it is proper to say that we understand poliomyelitis when we have isolated the responsible viruses and have identified the conditions under which they attack and cripple a person, but this is not *Verstehen*. That conception is an empathic, intuitive *feeling* of knowing a phenomenon from the inside, as it were. To take a more congenial example, we do not understand why a particular boy becomes delinquent from knowing that he comes from a neighborhood that an ecological survey has determined to be economically deprived and socially disorganized; whereas after we have read Farrell's *Studs Lonigan* and have seen such conditions and the embeddedness of delinquency in them portrayed with artistic power and vividness, then we understand (in the sense of *Verstehen*) the relation between these phenomena.

Holt used these examples to differentiate science and art. In contrast, we are suggesting that the two kinds of understanding are not incompatible but rather are each useful for different but equally laudable purposes. Difficulties arise only when one attempts to evaluate one approach according to the standards of the other. Thus, a formal statement such as $Y = 5.44X + 6.62$ has proven to be an extremely useful tool in the conceptualization and prediction of attraction responses. That formula plus the assumptions underlying it provide an abstract level of analysis with wide generality. If, however, one looks at such a formula with inappropriate expectations, he is doomed to disappointment. Such formal statements are not intended to describe the "actual" functioning of organisms. One student recently was puzzled as to how it was possible for subjects accurately and rapidly to calculate proportions, multiply the result by 5.44, add 6.62, and then make the appropriate check marks on the IJS. It is even more difficult for billiard balls to calculate their momentum and the angle at which they must bounce off the cushion so as not to behave erratically. Formal statements also are not designed to provide emotional insight in those examining them. One might stare at such a formula for a very long time without noting any connection between what is being described and his own inner experience in interpersonal interactions. When such expectancies are advanced inappropriately, it is not surprising that a formal theoretical model is viewed as sterile, mechanistic, dehumanizing, and all the rest.

On the other hand, a cognitively oriented description of a phenomenon tends to place one within the situation. By the use of analogy, anecdote, and artful word pictures, one can come to see "Oh yes, that's how it is. I've experienced that." Again, this sort of understanding is all the difference between knowing about something at the intellectual level and feeling it in one's viscera. Abelson (1968, p. 112) notes, "The danger in the easy conceptual appeal of consistency theories . . . is that systems of psycho-logic have not usually been specified in enough detail to render the subjective rationalist position potentially refutable." If one proposes to take descriptive material and make precise predictions, he is doomed to disappointment. These inappropriate expectations not surprisingly lead some to view cognitive descriptions as unscientific, vacuous, and useless.

It is proposed that the demands of science require both the formal theoretical systems characteristic of reinforcement theory and the intuitive understanding characteristic of cognitive theory. It is difficult to imagine a science beginning with mathematical equations and it is difficult to imagine a science terminating with artistic descriptions. The moral of the story is that neither the cognitive nor the reinforcement approach has a monopoly on TRUTH, and that each can be of unique value when used as conceptual tools and not as chauvinistic banners.

REFERENCES

Abelson, R. P. Psychological implication. In R. P. Abelson, E. Aronson, W. J. McGuire, T. M. Newcomb, M. J. Rosenberg, & P. H. Tannenbaum (eds.), *Theories of cognitive consistency: A sourcebook.* Chicago: Rand McNally, 1968, pp. 112-139.

Abelson, R. P., & Rosenberg, M. J. Symbolic psycho-logic: A model of attitudinal cognition. *Behavioral Science*, 1958, *3*, 1-13.

Anderson, N. H. A simple model for information integration. In R. P. Abelson et al (eds.), *Theories of cognitive consistency: A sourcebook*. Chicago: Rand McNally, 1968, pp. 731-743.

Aronson, E. Some antecedents of interpersonal attraction. In W. J. Arnold and D. Levine (eds.), *Nebraska symposium on motivation 1969*. Lincoln: University of Nebraska Press, 1970, pp. 143-173.

Brewer, R. E., & Brewer, M. B. Attraction and accuracy of perception in dyads. *Journal of Personality and Social Psychology*, 1968, *8*, 188-193.

Byrne, D. Interpersonal attraction and attitude similarity. *Journal of Abnormal and Social Psychology*, 1961, *62*, 713-715. (a)

Byrne, D. Interpersonal attraction as a function of affiliation need and attitude similarity. *Human Relations*, 1961, *3*, 283-289. (b)

Byrne, D. Response to attitude similarity-dissimilarity as a function of affiliation need. *Journal of Personality*, 1962, *30*, 164-177.

Byrne, D. Attitudes and attraction. In L. Berkowitz (ed.), *Advances in experimental social psychology*, Vol. 4. New York: Academic Press, 1969, pp. 35-89.

Byrne, D. The attraction paradigm. New York: Academic Press. In press.

Byrne, D., & Clore, G. L. Predicting interpersonal attraction toward strangers presented in three different stimulus modes. *Psychonomic Science*, 1966, *4*, 239-240.

Byrne, D., & Clore, G. L. Effectance arousal and attraction. *Journal of Personality and Social Psychology*, 1967, *6*, No. 4 (Whole No. 638).

Byrne, D., & Clore, G. L. A reinforcement model of evaluative responses. *Personality: An International Journal*, 1970, *1*, 103-128.

Byrne, D., & Ervin, C. R. Attraction toward a Negro stranger as a function of prejudice, attitude similarity, and the stranger's evaluation of the subject. *Human Relations*, 1969, *22*, 397-404.

Byrne, D,. Ervin, C. R., & Lamberth, J. Continuity between the experimental study of attraction and real life computer dating. *Journal of Personality and Social Psychology*, 1970, *16*, 157-165.

Byrne, D., & Griffitt, W. Similarity versus liking: A clarification. *Psychonomic Science*, 1966, *6*, 295-296.

Byrne, D., & Griffitt, W. Similarity and awareness of similarity of personality characteristics as determinants of attraction. *Journal of Experimental Research in Personality*, 1969, *3*, 179-186.

Byrne, D., Griffitt, W., & Clore, G. L. Attitudinal reinforcement effects as a function of stimulus homogeneity-heterogeneity. *Journal of Verbal Learning and Verbal Behavior*, 1968, *7*, 962-964.

Byrne, D., Griffitt, W., & Stefaniak, D. Attraction and similarity of personality characteristics. *Journal of Personality and Social Psychology*, 1967, *5*, 82-90.

Byrne, D., London, O., & Reeves, K. The effects of physical attractiveness, sex, and attitude similarity on interpersonal attraction. *Journal of Personality*, 1968, *36*, 259-271.

Byrne, D., & Nelson, D. Attraction as a linear function of proportion of positive reinforcements. *Journal of Personality and Social Psychology*, 1965, *1*, 659-663.

Byrne, D., & Rhamey, R. Magnitude of positive and negative reinforcements as a determinant of attraction. *Journal of Personality and Social Psychology*, 1965, *2*, 884-889.

Byrne, D., Young, R. K., & Griffitt, W. The reinforcement properties of attitude statements. *Journal of Experimental Research in Personality*, 1966, *1*, 266-276.

Cartwright, D., & Harary, F. Structural balance: A generalization of Heider's theory. *Psychological Review*, 1956, *63*, 277-293.

Clore, G. L. Discrimination learning as a function of awareness and magnitude of attitudinal reinforcement. Unpublished doctoral dissertation, University of Texas, 1966.

Clore, G. L., & Baldridge, B. The behavior of item weights in attitude-attraction research. *Journal of Experimental Social Psychology*, 1970, *6*, 177-186.

Festinger, L. A theory of social comparison processes. *Human Relations*, 1954, *7*, 117-140.

Golightly, C., & Byrne, D. Attitude statements as positive and negative reinforcements. *Science*, 1964, *146*, 798-799.

Gouaux, C. The effect of induced affective states on interpersonal attraction: A social motivational interpretation. Paper presented at the meeting of the Midwestern Psychological Association, Cincinnati, May, 1970. (a)

Gouaux, C. The influence of induced affective states on the effectiveness of social and non-social reinforcers in an instrumental learning task. Unpublished doctoral dissertation, Purdue University, 1970. (b)

Grant, D. A. Testing the null hypothesis and the strategy and tactics of investigating theoretical models. *Psychological Review*, 1962, *69*, 54-61.

Griffitt, W. Interpersonal attraction as a function of self-concept and personality similarity-dissimilarity. *Journal of Personality and Social Psychology*, 1966, *4*, 581-584.

Griffitt, W. Attraction toward a stranger as a function of direct and associated reinforcement. *Psychonomic Science*, 1968, *11*, 147-148.

Griffitt, W. Environmental effects on interpersonal affective behavior: Ambient effective temperature and attraction. *Journal of Personality and Social Psychology*, 1970, *15*, 240-244.

Griffitt, W., & Guay, P. "Object" evaluation and conditioned affect. *Journal of Experimental Research in Personality*, 1969, *4*, 1-8.

Heider, F. *The psychology of interpersonal relations*. New York: Wiley, 1958.

Holt, R. R. Individuality and generalization in the psychology of personality. *Journal of Personality*, 1962, *30*, 377-404.

Hull, C. L. *A behavior system*. New Haven: Yale University Press, 1952.

Jenkins, W. O. A temporal gradient of derived reinforcement. *American Journal of Psychology*, 1950, *63*, 237-243.

Kaplan, A. *The conduct of inquiry*. San Francisco: Chandler, 1964.

Kuhn, T. S. *The structure of scientific revolutions*. Chicago: University of Chicago Press, 1962.

Lamberth, J. The effect of sequential variables on performance using attitudinal stimuli. Unpublished doctoral dissertation, Purdue University, 1970.

Lamberth, J., & Craig, L. Differential magnitude of reward and magnitude shifts using attitudinal stimuli. *Journal of Experimental Research in Personality.* In press.

Lamberth, J., & Gay, R. A. Differential reward magnitude using a performance task and attitudinal stimuli. Paper read at the meeting of the Western Psychological Association, Vancouver, 1969.

Logan, F. A. The role of delay of reinforcement in determining reaction potential. *Journal of Experimental Psychology,* 1952, *43,* 393-399.

Lott, A. J. et al. The effect of delayed reward on the development of positive attitudes toward persons. *Journal of Experimental Social Psychology,* 1969, *5,* 101-113.

Lykken, D. T. Statistical significance in psychological research. *Psychological Bulletin,* 1968, *70,* 151-159.

Meehl, P. E. Theory-testing in psychology and physics: A methodological paradox. *Philosophy of Science,* 1967, *34,* 103-115.

Mueller, L. M. Interpersonal attraction as a function of inferred similarity-dissimilarity: A reversal effect. Unpublished doctoral dissertation, University of Texas, 1969.

Newcomb, T. M. Interpersonal balance. In R. P. Abelson et al (eds.), *Theories of cognitive consistency: A Sourcebook,* Chicago: Rand McNally, 1968, pp. 28-51.

Novak, D. W., & Lerner, M. J. Rejection as a consequence of perceived similarity. *Journal of Personality and Social Psychology,* 1968, *9,* 147-152.

Palmer, J. A. Vindiction, evaluation, and the effect of the stranger's competence on the attitude similarity-attraction function. Unpublished doctoral dissertation, University of Texas, 1969.

Reitz, W. E., Douey, J., & Mason, G. Role of homogeneity and centrality of attitude domain on reinforcing properties of attitude statements. *Journal of Experimental Research in Personality,* 1968, *3,* 120-125.

Rychlak, J. F. *A philosophy of science for personality theory.* Boston: Houghton Mifflin, 1968.

Senn, D. J. Attraction as a function of similarity-dissimilarity in task performance. Paper presented at the meeting of the Eastern Psychological Association, Atlantic City, April, 1970.

Taylor, H. F. *Balance in small groups.* New York: Van Nostrand Reinhold, 1970.

Underwood, B. J., & Keppel, G. One-trial learning? In N. J. Slamecka (ed.), *Human learning and memory.* New York: Oxford University Press, 1967, pp. 185-198.

5

Passionate Love

Elaine Walster

DEFINITIONS

Liking has been defined by a number of researchers (e.g., Newcomb, 1961; Homans, 1950) as "a positive attitude toward another, evidenced by a tendency to approach and interact with him." Theorists generally agree on the genesis of liking: individuals like those who reward them.*

Researchers have spent little time defining or investigating *passionate love*. Many theorists simply assume that passionate love is nothing more than very intense liking. We would argue, however, that passionate love is a distinct emotional state. We would argue that a person will experience love only if 1) he is physiologically aroused, and 2) he concludes that love is the appropriate label for his aroused feelings.

PASSIONATE LOVE: A TABOO TOPIC

Most of us would agree that passion is more fascinating than friendship. However, a multitude of researchers have conducted experiments on liking, while very few have explored passionate love.

This report was financed by National Institute of Mental Health Grant MH 16661 and National Science Foundation Grant GS 2932. The theoretical framework I present was developed in collaboration with Dr. Ellen Berscheid, University of Minnesota.

* We use the term *companionate love* to indicate unusually intense *liking* between two persons.

What accounts for this imbalance?

1) First, scientists who wanted to investigate romantic attraction found it very difficult to secure research funds. Granting agencies, sensitive to the feelings of legislators and the public, were nervous about even considering proposals whose titles contained the offensive words "Love" or "Sex." Even today, whenever a researcher is ill-mannered enough to affix such a title to his proposal, alert bureaucrats quickly expurgate the offensive term and substitute the euphemism, "social affiliation."

2) Psychologists did not themselves acknowledge the legitimacy of investigating passionate love. They often ridiculed colleagues who began conducting experiments on this taboo topic. To study love was to be "soft-headed," "unscientific," or to possess a flair for the trivial. It is interesting to note that early in their careers some of our most eminent social psychologists conducted one—and only one—study on romantic attraction. Professional reaction to their research uniformly led them to decide to investigate other topics.

3) Psychologists tend to assume that in the laboratory one can only study mild and quickly developing phenomena. Although poets argue that love may occur "at first sight," psychologists have had less confidence that one can generate passionate love in a two-hour laboratory experiment. Thus, many researchers erroneously assumed that passionate love could only be studied in the field.

Suddenly, the situation changed. The humanists invaded psychology, and the study of tender emotions became respectable. Masters and Johnson's (1966) impressive research demonstrated that even sex could be examined in the laboratory. (Ironically, these pioneers were attacked by the public for failing to investigate love as well as sex.) In the last five years more psychologists have begun to study romantic love than investigated the phenomenon in the history of psychology.

The problem now is not finding respectability but finding out some facts. Presently, when faced with requests for information about love and sex, chagrined psychologists must admit that "they really don't know love at all." Hopefully, in this conference we can gain a better understanding about this vital—and entertaining—topic. In this lecture, I will propose a theoretical framework which may give us a better understanding of passionate love.

"WHAT IS THIS THING CALLED LOVE?"

Interpersonal attraction and companionate love seem like sensible phenomena. One can predict quite well how much a person will like another, if he knows to what extent the other rewards or punishes the person. Reward has so predictable an impact on liking that Byrne et al (1968) could with confidence propose an exact correspondence between reinforcement and liking: ("Attraction towards X is a positive linear function of the proportion of positive reinforcements received from X or expected from X.") Data support their formulation.

Sometimes passionate love seems to operate in a sensible fashion. Some practical people have been known to fall in love with those beautiful, wise, entertaining, and kind people who offer affection or material rewards to them. Generally, however, passionate love does not seem to fit so neatly into the reinforcement paradigm. Individuals do *not* always feel passionate about the person who provides the most rewards with the greatest consistency. Passion sometimes develops under conditions that would seem more likely to provoke aggression and hatred than love. For example, reinforcement theorists argue that "we like those who like us and reject those who dislike us." Yet individuals experience intense love for those who have rejected them.

A woman discovers her husband is seeing another. The pain and suffering the jealous wife experiences at this discovery cause her to realize how much she loves her husband.

Lovers pine away for the girls who spurn their affection. For example, a recent Associated Press release reports the desperate excuse of an Italian lover who kidnapped his former sweetheart: " 'The fact that she rejected me only made me want and love her more,' he tearfully explained."

Reinforcement theorists tell us that "frustration always breeds aggression." Yet, inhibited sexuality is assumed to be the foundation of romantic feelings. Freud (1912) even argued that:

Some obstacle is necessary to swell the tide of libido to its height; and at all periods of history whenever natural barriers in the way of satisfaction have not sufficed, mankind has erected conventional ones in order to enjoy love.

The observation that passionate love flourishes in settings which would seem to thwart its development has always been puzzling to social scientists. Poets attribute such inexplicable phenomena to the essential illogic of love. Scientists, who refuse to acknowledge that anything is inexplicable, do not have such an easy way out.

Happily, we believe that a theoretical framework exists which makes the "illogical" phenomena of passionate love explicable and predictable.

SCHACHTER'S TWO-COMPONENT THEORY

On the basis of an ingenious series of experiments, Schachter (1964) proposed a paradigm for understanding human emotional response. He argues that in order for a person to experience true emotion, two factors must coexist: 1) The individual must be physiologically aroused, and 2) It must be reasonable to interpret his stirred-up state in emotional terms. Schachter argued that neither physiological arousal nor appropriate cognitions *alone* is sufficient to produce an emotional experience.

It is possible to manipulate an individual's physiological arousal artificially. A drug, adrenalin, exists whose effects mimic the discharge of the sympathetic nervous system. Shortly after one receives an injection of adrenalin, systolic blood pressure increases markedly, heart rate increases somewhat, cutaneous blood flow decreases, muscle and cerebral blood flow increase, blood sugar and lactic acid concentration increase, and respiration rate increases slightly. The individual who has been injected with adrenalin experiences palpitation, tremor, and sometimes flushing and accelerated breathing. These reactions are identical to the physiological reactions which accompany a variety of natural emotional states.

An injection of adrenalin will not, by itself, however, engender an emotional response in a person. When an individual is injected with adrenalin and asked to introspect, he will report either no emotional response or, at best, report feeling "as if" he might be experiencing some emotion (Marañon, 1924). Individuals make statements such as "I feel *as if* I were afraid." The person who has been injected with adrenalin perceives that something is not quite authentic about his reactions. Something is missing.

Schachter argues that what is missing is an appropriate label for the physiological reactions one is experiencing. If one could lead the drugged individual to attribute his stirred-up state to some emotion-arousing event (rather than attributing it to the injection of adrenalin which he received), Schachter argues that he would experience a "true" emotion.

The researcher who wishes to test the notion that physiological arousal and appropriate cognitions are separate and indispensable components of a true emotional experience, is faced with the challenging task of separately manipulating these two components. In a classic study, Schachter and Singer (1962) conceived of a way to do just that. Volunteers were recruited for an experiment which the experimenters claimed was designed to investigate the effects of a new vitamin compound, Suproxin, on vision.

Manipulating Physiological Arousal: Volunteers were injected with a substance which was identified as Suproxin. Actually, one half of the students were injected with epinephrine ($\frac{1}{2}$ cc of a 1:1000 solution of Winthrop Laboratory's Suprarenin). Such an injection causes the intense physiological reactions described earlier. One half received a placebo ($\frac{1}{2}$ cc of saline solution).

Manipulating an Appropriate Explanation: Schachter wished to lead some of the volunteers to correctly attribute their physiological state to a nonemotional cause (the injection). He wished to lead others to attribute their stirred-up state to an emotional cause.

Thus, in one condition, (the *Non-Emotional Attribution* condition), individuals were given a complete explanation of how the shot would affect them. They were warned that in 15 to 20 minutes the injection of "Suproxin" would cause palpitation, tremor, etc. Presumably, when students began to experience these symptoms, they could properly attribute their stirred-up state to the shot and would *not* attribute their excitement to the activities in which they were engaging at the time the adrenalin began to take effect.

In the *Emotional Attribution* conditions, things were arranged to *discharge* students from attributing their stirred-up state to the shot. One group of volunteers was given no information about possible side effects of the shot. A second group of volunteers was deliberately misled as to the potential side effects of the shot. It was assumed that volunteers who received either no information or incorrect information would be unlikely to attribute their tremors and palpitations to the shot. After all, these symptoms took 20 minutes to develop. Instead, the authors hoped that volunteers would attribute their arousal to whatever they happened to be doing when the drug took effect. The authors then arranged things so that what volunteers "happened to be doing" was participating in either a gay, happy, social interaction or participating in a tense, explosive interaction.

If the subject had been assigned to the *Euphoria* condition, his fellow student (who was actually a confederate) had been trained to generate excitement while they waited 20 minutes for the experiment to begin. As soon as the experimenter left the room, the confederate began "acting up." He shot paper wads into the wastebasket, built a paper tower which he sent crashing to the floor and generally kidded around.

In the *Anger* setting, the confederate had been trained to make the subject angry. The confederate first complained about the experimental procedures. He became especially indignant on encountering the questionnaire they had been asked to fill out (and which admittedly asked stupid and offensive questions). Finally, the confederate slammed his questionnaire to the floor and stomped out.

The authors assessed subject's emotional reactions to the confederate's behavior in two ways. Observers stationed behind a one-way mirror assessed to what extent the subject caught the stooge's euphoric or angry mood; secondly, subjects were asked to describe their moods and to estimate how euphoric and angry they felt.

Schachter and Singer predicted that those subjects who had received an adrenalin injection would have stronger emotional reactions than would subjects who had received a placebo or had received an adrenalin injection but had been warned of exactly what physiological changes they should expect. The data supported these hypotheses. The experiment thus supported the contention that both physiological arousal and appropriate cognitions are indispensable components of a true emotional experience. Schachter and Wheeler (1962) and Hohmann (1962) provide additional support for this contention.

THE TWO-COMPONENT THEORY AND PASSIONATE LOVE

The discovery that almost any sort of intense physiological arousal—if properly interpreted—will precipitate an emotional experience has intriguing implications. We were particularly intrigued by the possibility that Schachter's "two-component" theory might help explain a heretofore inexplicable phenomena—passionate love.

As long as researchers were busily absorbed in figuring out how passionate love could be integrated into the reinforcement paradigm, we made little progress. The observation that negative experiences often lead to increased evaluation remained inexplicable.

A sudden insight solved our dilemma. Two components are necessary for a passionate experience: arousal and appropriate cognitions. Perhaps negative experiences do not increase love by somehow improving one's evaluation of the other (beneficially altering his cognitions). Perhaps negative experiences are effective in inducing love because they intensify the second component—arousal.

We would suggest that perhaps it does not really matter how one pro-

duces an agitated state in an individual. Stimuli that usually produce sexual arousal, gratitude, anxiety, guilt, loneliness, hatred, jealousy, or confusion may all increase one's physiological arousal, and thus increase the intensity of his emotional experience. As long as one attributes his agitated state to passion, he should experience true passionate love. As soon as he ceases to attribute his tumultuous feelings to passion, love should die.

Does any evidence exist to support our contention? Some early observers noticed that any form of strong emotional arousal breeds love (although not, of course, interpreting this relationship in Schachterian terms). Finck (1891), an early psychologist, concluded:

Love can only be excited by strong and vivid emotion, and it is almost immaterial whether these emotions are agreeable or disagreeable. The Cid wooed the proud heart of Diana Ximene, whose father he had slain, by shooting one after another of her pet pigeons. Such persons as arouse in us only weak emotions or none at all, are obviously least likely to incline us toward them. . . . Our aversion is most likely to be bestowed on individuals who, as the phrase goes, are neither 'warm' nor 'cold'; whereas impulsive, choleric people, though they may readily offend us, are just as capable of making us warmly attached to them (p. 240).

Unfortunately, experimental evidence does not yet exist to support the contention that almost any form of high arousal, if properly labeled, will deepen passion. There are, however, a few studies designed to test other hypotheses, which provide some minimal support for our contention.*

Since it was the juxtaposition of misery and ecstasy in romantic love that we initially found so perplexing, let us first examine the relation between negative experiences and love.

Unpleasant Emotional States: Facilitators of Passion?

That negative reinforcements produce strong emotional reactions in all animals is not in doubt (see Skinner, 1938). There is some evidence that under the right conditions such unpleasant, but arousing, states as fear, rejection, and frustration do enhance romantic passion.

---

* These studies are only "minimally supportive" because the authors investigate only liking, not passionate loving—a phenomenon we have argued is unique. Whether or not the same results would occur in a romantic context must yet be determined.

Fear: A Facilitator of Passion

Frightening a person is a very good way of producing intense psychological arousal for a substantial period of time (see Ax, 1953; Wolf and Wolff, 1947; and Schachter, 1957).

An intriguing study by Brehm et al (1970) demonstrates that a frightened man is a romantic man. Brehm et al tested the hypothesis that "a person's attraction to another would be multiplied by prior arousal from an irrelevant event." In this experiment, some men were led to believe that they would soon receive three "pretty stiff" electrical shocks. Half of the men, "Threat" subjects, were allowed to retain this erroneous expectation throughout the experiment. Half of the men, "Threat-Relief," were frightened and then, sometime later, were told that the experimenter had made an error; they had been assigned to the control group and would receive no shock. The remainder of the men were assigned to a control group, in which the possibility of their receiving shock was not even mentioned.

Men were then introduced to a young co-ed, and asked how much they liked her.

The Threat subjects who expected to be shocked in the future should be quite frightened at the time they meet the girl. The Threat-Relief subjects who had just learned they would not be shocked should be experiencing vast relief when they meet the girl. Both the frightened and the frightened-relieved men should be more aroused than are men in the control group. Brehm predicted, as we would, that Threat and Threat-Relief subjects would like the girl more than would control subjects. Brehm's expectations were confirmed; threatened men experienced more liking for the girl (and did not differ in their liking) than did control group men, who had never been frightened. An irrelevant frightening event, then, does seem to facilitate attraction.

Rejection: An Antecedent of Passion

Rejection is always disturbing. And generally when a person is rejected he has a strong emotional reaction. Usually he experiences embarrassment, pain, or anger. Although it is probably most reasonable for a rejected person to label his agitation in this way, if our hypothesis is correct, it should be possible, under the right conditions, to induce a rejected individual to label his emotional response as "love" as well as "hate."

Some slight evidence that passionate love *or* hate may emerge from rejection comes from several laboratory experiments designed to test other hypotheses (Dittes, 1959; Walster, 1965; and Jacobs et al, 1971).

Let us consider one of these experiments and the way a Schachterian might reinterpret these data.

The experiment of Jacobs et al was designed to determine how changes in the self-esteem of college students affected their receptivity to love and affection. First, students took a number of personality tests (the *MMPI,* Rorschach, etc.) A few weeks later, a psychologist returned an analysis of his personality to each student. Half of the students were given a flattering personality report. The reports stressed their sensitivity, honesty, originality, and freedom of outlook. (Undoubtedly this flattering personality report confirmed many of the wonderful things the students already thought about themselves.) Half of the students received an insulting personality report. The report stressed their immaturity, weak personality, conventionality, and lack of leadership ability. This critical report was naturally most upsetting for students.

Soon after receiving their analyses, the males got acquainted individually with a young female college student (actually, this girl was an experimental confederate). Half of the time the girl treated the boy in a warm, affectionate, and accepting way. Under such conditions, the men who had received the critical personality evaluation were far more attracted to her than were their more confident counterparts. (Presumably, the previous irrelevant arousal engendered by rejection facilitated the subsequent development of affection.)

Half of the time the girl was cold and rejecting. Under these conditions, a dramatic reversal occurred; the previously rejected men disliked the girl more than did their more confident counterparts. (Presumably, under these conditions, the low self-esteem individual's agitation was transformed to hatred.)

An irrelevant, painful event, then, can incite various strong emotional reactions toward others. Depending on how he labels his feelings, the individual may experience either intensive attraction or intense hostility.

Frustration and Challenge: Facilitators of Passion

Socrates, Ovid, Terence, the Kama Sutra and "Dear Abby" are all in agreement about one thing: the person whose affection is easily won will inspire less passion than the person whose affection is hard to win.

Vassilikos (1964) poetically elucidated the principle that frustration fuels passion while continual gratification dims it:

Once upon a time there was a little fish who was a bird from the waist up and who was madly in love with a little bird who was a fish from the waist up. So the Fish-Bird kept saying to the Bird-Fish: "Oh, why were we created so that we can never live together? You in the wind and I in the wave. What a pity for both of us." And the Bird-Fish would answer: "No, what luck for both of us. This way we'll always be in love because we'll always be separated" (p. 131).

Some provisional evidence that the hard-to-get person may engender unusual passion in the eventually successful suitor comes from Aronson and Linder (1965). These authors tested the hypothesis that: "A gain in esteem is a more potent reward than invariant esteem." They predicted that a person would be better liked if his positive regard was difficult to acquire than if it was easily had.

This hypothesis was tested in the following way: Subjects were required to converse with a confederate (who appeared to be another naive subject) over a series of seven meetings. After each meeting, the subject discovered (secretly) how her conversation partner felt about her. How the confederate "felt" was systematically varied. In one condition the girl expressed a negative impression of the subject after their first meetings. (She described the subject as being a dull conversationalist, a rather ordinary person, not very intelligent, as probably not having many friends, etc.). Only after the partners had become well acquainted did she begin expressing favorable opinions of the subject. In the remaining conditions, from the first, the confederate expressed only positive opinions about the subject.

As Aronson and Linder predicted, subjects liked the confederate whose affection was hard to win better than they liked the confederate whose high opinion was readily obtained.

The preceding evidence is consistent with our suggestion that under the right conditions, a hard-to-get girl should generate more passion than the constantly rewarding girl. The aloof girl's challenge may excite the suitor; her momentary rejection may shake his self-esteem. In both cases, such arousal may intensify the suitor's feelings toward her.

The preceding analysis lends some credence to the argument that the juxtaposition of agony and ecstasy in passionate love is not entirely accidental. (The original meaning of "passion" was, in fact, "agony"— for example, as in Christ's passion.) Loneliness, deprivation, frustration, hatred, and insecurity may in fact supplement a person's romantic experiences. Passion requires physiological arousal, and all of the preceding states are certainly arousing.

Pleasant Emotional States: Facilitators of Passion?

We would like to make it clear that, theoretically, passion need not include a negative component. The positive reinforcements of discovery, excitement, companionship, and playful-joy can generate as intense an arousal as that stirred by fear, frustration, or rejection. For example, in many autobiographical accounts, entirely joyful (albeit brief) passionate encounters are described (e.g., Duncan, 1968).

Sexual Gratification: A Facilitator of Passion

Sexual experiences can be enormously rewarding and enormously arousing. Masters and Johnson (1966) point out that sexual intercourse induces hyperventilation, tachycardia, and marked increases in blood pressure. And, religious advisors, school counselors, and psychoanalysts to the contrary—sexual gratification has undoubtedly generated as much passionate love as has sexual continence.

Valins (1966) demonstrated that even the erroneous belief that another has excited one (sexually or aesthetically) will facilitate attraction. Valins recruited male college students for a study of males' physiological reactions to sexual stimuli. The sexual stimuli he utilized were ten semi-nude *Playboy* photographs. The subjects were told that while they scrutinized these photographs, their heart rate would be amplified and recorded. They were led to believe that their heart rates altered markedly to some of the slides but that they had no reaction at all to others. (Valins assumed that the subjects would interpret an alteration in heart rate as sexual enthusiasm.)

The subjects' liking for the "arousing" and "nonarousing" slides was then assessed in three ways. Regardless of the measure used, the men markedly preferred the pin-ups they thought had aroused them to those that had not affected their heart rate. 1) They were asked to rate how "attractive or appealing" each pin-up was. They preferred the pin-ups they believed were arousing to all others. 2) They were offered a pin-up in renumeration for participating in the experiment. They chose the arousing pin-ups more often than the nonarousing ones. 3) Finally, they were interviewed a month later (in a totally different context) and they still markedly preferred the arousing pin-ups to the others.

Need Satisfaction: A Facilitator of Passion

Although psychologists tend to focus almost exclusively on the contribution of sex to love, other rewards can have an equally important emotional impact. People have a wide variety of needs, and at any stage of life many of one's needs must remain unsatisfied. When any important unsatisfied need is recognized or met, the emotional response which accompanies such reinforcement could provide fuel for passion. To the adolescent boy who has been humored, coddled, and babied at home, the girl who finally recognizes his masculinity may be an over-powering joy. The good, steady, reliable, hard-working father may be captivated when an alert lady recognizes that he has the potential to be a playful and reckless lover.

To the person who has been deprived of such rewards, an intelligent, artistic, witty, beautiful, athletic, or playful companion may prove a passionate and absorbing joy.

LABELING

We are proposing a two-factor theory of passionate love. Yet the preceding discussion has focused almost exclusively on one factor. We have concentrated on demonstrating that physiological arousal is a crucial component of passionate love, and that fear, pain, and frustration as well as discovery and delight may contribute to the passionate experience.

We should now at least remind the reader that according to our theory an individual will be incapable of experiencing "love" unless he's prepared to define his feelings in that way.

Cultural Encouragement of Love

In our culture, it is expected that everyone will eventually fall in love. Individuals are strongly encouraged to interpret a wide range of confused feelings as love. Linton makes this point in a somewhat harsh observation:

> All societies recognize that there are occasional violent emotional attachments between persons of the opposite sex, but our present American culture is practically the only one which has attempted to capitalize on these and make them the basis for marriage. The hero of the modern American movie is always a romantic lover, just as the hero of an old Arab epic is always an epileptic. A cynic may suspect that in any ordinary population the percentage of individuals with capacity for romantic love of the Hollywood type was about as large as that of persons able to throw genuine epileptic fits (p.175).

* From: *The study of man: An introduction,* by Ralph Linton. Copyright 1936. Copyright © 1964 by Meredith Corporation. Reprinted by permission of Appleton-Century-Crofts, Educational Division, Meredith Corporation.

Individuals are often encouraged to interpret certain confused or mixed feelings as love, because our culture insists that certain reactions are acceptable if one is madly in love. For example, the delightful experience of sexual intercourse can be frankly labeled as "sexual fun" by a man. Such an interpretation of what she is experiencing is probably less acceptable to his partner. She (and her parents) are undoubtedly happier if she attributes her abandoned behavior to love.

Margaret Mead interprets jealousy in one way:

> Jealousy is not a barometer by which the depth of love may be read. It merely records the degree of the lover's insecurity. It is a negative, miserable state of feeling, having its origin in a sense of insecurity and inferiority.

Jealous people, however, usually interpret their jealous reactions in quite another way; jealous feelings are taken as evidence of passionate love rather than inferiority. Thus, in this culture, a jealous man is a loving man rather than an embarrassed man.

Thus, whether or not an individual is susceptible to "falling in love," should depend on the expectations of his culture and his reference groups.

Individual Expectations

An individual's own expectations should also determine how likely he is to experience love.

The individual who thinks of himself as a nonromantic person should fall in love less often than should an individual who assumes that love is inevitable. The nonromantic may experience the same feelings that the romantic does, but he will code them differently.

Similarly, individuals who feel they are unlovable should have a difficult time finding love. Individuals convey their expectations in very subtle ways to others, and these expectations influence the way one's partner labels *his* reactions. The insecure girl who complains to her boyfriend: "You don't love me, you just think you do. If you loved me you wouldn't treat me this way," and then itemizes evidence of his neglect, may, by automatically interpreting her boyfriend's actions in a damaging way, effect an alteration in his feelings for her. Alternately, a girl with a great deal of self-confidence, may (by her unconscious guidance) induce a normally unreceptive gentleman to label his feelings for her as love.

REFERENCES

Aronson, E., & Linder, D. Gain and loss of esteem as determinants of interpersonal attractiveness. *Journal of Experimental Social Psychology,* 1965, *1,* 156-171.

Ax, A. F. Fear and anger in humans. *Psychosomatic Medicine,* 1953, *15,* 433-442.

Brehm, J. W., Gatz, M., Geothals, G., McCrimmon, J., & Ward, L. Psychological arousal and interpersonal attraction. Mimeo, 1970, Available from authors.

Byrne, D., London, O., & Reeves K. The effect of physical attractiveness, sex, and attitude similarity on interpersonal attraction. *Journal of Personality,* 1968, *36,* 269-271.

Dittes, J. E. Attractiveness of group as function of self-esteem and acceptance by group. *Journal of Abnormal and Social Psychology,* 1959, *59,* 77-82.

Duncan, I. *Isadora.* New York: Award Books, 1968.

Finck, H. T. *Romantic love and personal beauty: Their development, causal relations, historic and national peculiarities.* London: Macmillan, 1891.

Freud, S. The most prevalent form of degradation in erotic life. In E. Jones (ed.), *Collected papers, 4.* London: Hogarth, 1925, pp. 203-216.

Hohmann, G. W. The effect of dysfunctions of the autonomic nervous system on experienced feelings and emotions. Paper read at Conference on Emotions and Feelings at New School for Social Research, New York, 1962.

Homans, G. C. *The human group.* New York: Harcourt, Brace, and World, 1950.

Jacobs, L., Walster, E., & Berscheid, E. Self-esteem and attraction. *Journal of Personality and Social Psychology,* 1971, *17,* 84-91.

Linton, R. *The study of man* (1936). New York: Appleton-Century, 1964.

Maranon, G. Contribution a l'etude de l'action emotive de l'adrenaline. *Revue Francaise Endocrinalogia,* 1924, *2,* 301-325.

Masters, W. H., & Johnson, V. E. *Human sexual response.* Boston: Little, Brown and Company, 1966.

Mead, M. In A. M. Krich, *The anatomy of love.* New York: Dell, 1960.

Newcomb, T. N. *The acquaintance process.* New York: Holt, Rinehart, and Winston, 1961.

Schachter, J. Pain, fear and anger in hypertensives and normotensives: A psychophysiological study. *Psychosomatic Medicine,* 1957, *19,* 17-24.

Schachter, S. The interaction of cognitive and physiological determinants of emotional state. In Berkowitz (ed.), *Advances in experimental social psychology, 1.* New York: Academic Press, 1964, pp. 49-80.

Schachter, S., & Singer, J. Cognitive, social and physiological determinants of emotional state. *Psychological Review,* 1962, *69,* 379-399.

Schachter, S., & Wheeler, L. Epinephrine, chlorpromazine, and amusement. *Journal of Abnormal Social Psychology,* 1962, *65,* 121-128.

Valins, S. Cognitive effects of false heart-rate feedback. *Journal of Personality and Social Psychology,* 1966, *4,* 400-408.

Vassilikos, V. *The plant; the well; the angel: A trilogy.* Translated from Greek by Edmund and Mary Keeley (1st American ed.). New York: Knopf, 1964.

Walster, E. The effect of self-esteem on romantic liking. *Journal of Experimental Social Psychology*, 1965, *1*, 184-197.

Wolf, S., & Wolff, H. G. *Human gastric function* (2nd edition). London: Oxford University Press, 1947.

6

A Theory of Marital Choice and
Its Applicability to
Marriage Adjustment

Bernard I. Murstein

ANTECEDENTS OF MODERN THEORY

It is scarcely possible to speak of theories of marital choice in the West before the nineteenth century. Traditionally, prior to this time, the choice had been made by parents either for political or economic considerations or because of the affinity the parents saw in the *parents* of the intended spouse of their offspring. However, America, from its inception, had carried over from Europe the spirit of self-determination in marital choice as well as in politics and religion. Europe also, spurred on by the romantic movement of the late eighteenth and early nineteenth centuries, had evolved a concept of "love" marriages.

A review of early marriage manuals in the United States reveals, nevertheless, that "love" was not conceptualized in the same manner as it generally is today. As a British observer noted, "Love, among the American people, appears to be regarded rather as an affair of the judgment, than of the heart; its expression seems to spring from a sense of duty, rather than from a sentiment of feeling" (Buckingham, 1867, p. 479). An individual loved as a function of his role as spouse rather than because of the quality of interaction between him and his beloved; hence love was more properly seen as unfolding after marriage rather than before it.

In their review of nineteenth century marriage manuals, Gordon and Bernstein (1969) further observe that the chief criteria of mate-choice were religious, constitutional and physical, and moral and character considerations. An ideal husband, for example, was religious, sound of wind and limb, and the recipient of no black marks for ". . . idleness, intemperate use of intoxicating drinks, smoking, chewing, sniffing tobacco . . . taking . . . opium, licentiousness . . ., gambling, swearing and keeping late hours at night" (Fowler, 1855, p. 131). Love was characterized, therefore, by an appreciation of the other's sterling qualities. Nowhere in early nineteenth century treatises, was there much emphasis on love resulting from the quality of interaction of the man and woman.

In 1821, however, Hegel published his *The Philosophy of Right* which, though hardly a marriage manual, did treat of the interaction of forces. As a result of his dialectics, Hegel held that two opposite forces interact to form a new more viable entity.

The force of generation, as of mind, is all the greater, the greater the apposition out of which it is reproduced. Familiarity, close acquaintance, the habit of common pursuits, should not precede marriage, they should come about for the first time within it. And their development has all the more value, the richer it is and the more facets it has (Hegel, 1952, p. 134).

Some time later, Herbert Spencer became one of the first to note the relation of love to the ideal. In a letter to a male friend about to be married, he remarked that "the true sentiment of love between man and woman arises from each serving as the representative of the other's ideal" (Spencer 1926, p. 267).

During the second half of the nineteenth century, articles on marriage followed Hegel's and Spencer's suit and dealt increasingly with interactions between men and women. In this they were influenced by the effects of industrialization which freed the middle-class woman from exceedingly tedious household tasks and allowed more time for the "luxury" of interaction not related to the sex-role tasks each was expected to perform.

O. S. Fowler devoted a considerable number of pages of his book, *Matrimony*, to this new problem of compatibility. He maintained stoutly that like must marry like. Turning to nature for support he asked, "Do lions naturally associate with sheep, or wolves with fowls, or ele-

phants with tigers?" (Fowler 1859, p. 280). Nature, nevertheless, was
not rigidly bound to the principle of similarity. According to Fowler,
when Nature saw one of her subjects depart drastically from the norm, she
created in that person a powerful attraction for an opposite type; the
exceedingly tall, thin man, therefore, was drawn to the short, plumpish
woman. The same principle held for temperament and mental ability.
A man with a magnificent memory but fuzzy conceptual powers ought
to marry a woman with superb conceptual powers but a weak memory.
The children, Fowler assures us, will have both conceptual strength and
a marvelous memory.*

The basic principle of marital choice could be summed up thusly:
"Wherein, and as far as you are what you ought to be, marry one *like*
yourself; but wherein and as far as you have any marked *excesses* or
defects, marry those *unlike* yourself in these objectionable particulars"
(Fowler, 1859, p. 295).

The concept of complementarity spread rapidly toward the close of
the century, and Allen (1886) maintained, as did *Chamber's Journal*
(1898), that "We fall in love with our moral, mental, and physical com-
plement." There was no need for scientific match-making to guide the
principals in a marriage, however, since in the opinion of at least one
scientist, evolution automatically took care of the problem (Campbell,
1886). Coan (1869) agreed with the thesis of complementarity as concerns "natural organization," by which he meant temperament and
physique, but he added that, in terms of learned behavior there must
be similarity in purpose and thought; thus, "The secret of fitness of
marriage is *opposition of temperament with identity of aim*" (Coan,
1869, p. 500).

It was one thing to talk of the need for complementarity and quite
another to be able to diagnose its presence. We know today that "dating"
behavior is often a poor predictor of marital behavior. In the nineteenth
century, the task of assessing the potential partner's temperament must
have been infinitely more difficult. Chaperones were often present when
the couple were together, and physical mobility was much more limited
than today. Courting behavior was more artificial, and the underlying
traits of an individual more difficult to assess.

---

* Fowler, like a famous dancer of the succeeding century, seems not to have considered
the other possibility. This dancer, renowned for her beauty and physical grace but
not for her mental strength, proposed to George Bernard Shaw, renowned for his
wit but not for his physique, that they have a child. The offspring, she claimed,
would inherit his wit and her body. Shaw reflected a moment and then wondered
out loud whether the child might not have his body and her wit. The child was
never conceived.

Fortunately, a budding science, phrenology, obviated the need for interaction. Originally formulated by Franz Joseph Gall around 1800, phrenology stated that man's character and talent are localized in specific portions of his brain. The size and development of the regions are proportionate to the development of the particular faculty and cause corresponding changes in the skull; hence, from an examination of the lumps and crevices of the scalp, an experienced phrenologist can make an accurate assessment of personality.

In the posterior regions of the brain lay the areas related to marriage. As listed by Wells (1869) , they included Amativeness, Conjugality, and Inhabitiveness. The first is responsible for sexual activity, the second for "the mating propensity or instinct for permanent union" (Wells, 1869, p. 11) , and the last for the love of home. Physiognomy also played a role, so that, for example, a protruding jaw was a sure sign of sexual strength, whereas a dullard was diagnosed readily enough by the fact that his forehead was shorter in vertical length than his nose. A person with a feebly sized cerebellum (believed to be the seat of Amativeness) ought never to marry, and phrenologists did not hesitate to advise clients to break their engagements if they found this important element wanting in their fiancé (e) . Although phrenology has been wholly discredited today, its hold on the nineteenth century public was so great that even Queen Victoria did not hesitate to have the royal children's heads examined by a phrenologist (Turner, 1954) .

In sum, we may conclude that nineteenth century thinking held that a couple should be homogamously selected with respect to the traditional cultural variables such as education, wealth, and religion. Regarding "temperament," there was some division between the advocates of total complementarity and those calling for similarity for "good" traits and complementarity for deviations from the norm.

THEORIES OF THE TWENTIETH CENTURY

The twentieth century witnessed the removal of much of the legal, political and economic discrimination against women. It was inevitable, therefore, that women should exercise these newfound powers in their choice of a spouse. No longer as fearful of economic insecurity, they now focused more on the qualities of the relationship than on the mere occupational capability of the man and his freedom from noxious habits. To a lesser degree, the same was true of men. As modern household machines become part of everyday living, and as the populace shifted to the cities, the physical and domestic skills of the wife became less crucial, and her companionship capability increased in importance.

Despite their greater emphasis on the interaction between the couple, the new theories differed considerably among themselves on the dimensions of marital choice. One such dimension is consciousness of the criteria for selection. In general, the psychoanalytic school has held that the criteria are unconscious. Kubie (1956), for example, believes on that account that the process of marital choice is unamenable to scientific study. Jung (Evans, 1964) believed that the search for a mate was guided by unconscious archetypes. In each man, this archetype of the feminine is called the *anima*. In Jung's own words, "You see that girl, or at least a good imitation of your type, and instantly you get the seizure; you are caught. And afterward you may discover that it was a hell of a mistake" (Evans, 1964, pp. 51-52).

Freud (1957) presented two types of marital choice. The human being, in his view, originally possesses two sexual objects. One is himself, the other the woman who tends him. With age, these object-choices divide. Love involving the search for a substitute mother is called *anaclitic* (dependency) love, and the love that takes itself as the object is called *narcissistic*. For reasons not explained, men are more apt to be the anaclitic type, whereas women are the narcissistic type. This is not a hard and fast rule, however, because there are examples of female anaclitics and male narcissists. Within each of these types, there are several paths to object choice.

A person may love:

1) According to the narcissistic type:
   a) What he himself is (i.e., himself)
   b) What he himself was
   c) What he himself would like to be
   d) Someone who was once part of himself

2) According to the anaclitic (attachment) type:
   a) The woman who feeds him
   b) The man who protects him (Freud, 1957, p. 90)

Psychoanalysts have done little or no research on verifying these or other psychoanalytic concepts, focusing instead on a narrow range of middle and upper-class couples who were already married and experiencing personal and marital maladjustment. What little effort has been expended in testing psychoanalytic beliefs regarding marital choice has been largely undertaken by sociologists who have focused on the Oedipal and Electra choice patterns. These efforts (Mangus, 1936; Kirkpatrick, 1937; Winch, 1951) have not confirmed psychoanalytic theory.

At the other end of the continuum lies the concept of marital choice as a consciously experienced effort. The individual is said to possess an image of an ideal-spouse which he seeks to implement with a real person who approaches this ideal as much as possible. The ideal might be highly idiosyncratic or largely determined by societal or subgroup norms. The most quoted study in this respect is that by Anselm Strauss (1946). His sample consisted of 373 college level, white Chicagoans who either were engaged or recently married, and who filled out a questionnaire about their ideal and actual partners. Supplementary information came from interview data of 50 additional, similar subjects.

Strauss found that 80 per cent of his subjects reported that they had held an ideal of a spouse, and only 14.5 per cent thought their ideals were unconscious. About half reported comparing their actual partner and ideal when deciding on a choice, and half did not. Some 59 per cent achieved their physical ideal and 74 per cent their personality ideal.

The influence of an ideal-spouse image has been rejected by Udry (1965) in a study of 90 engaged college subjects. However, serious conceptual and methodological flaws, which space does not permit discussing further, vitiate the force of his conclusions. Even so, objection can be raised to Strauss' findings. Can one rely on the testimony that the image guided choice *before* the spouse was selected, or was it rather the case that a vague, unutilizable image was clarified by simply taking on the qualities of the flesh and blood partners? The influence of the ideal on marital choice, therefore, awaits future research.

SOCIOLOGY OF MARITAL CHOICE

By far the greatest amount of research in marital choice has been done by sociologists. A division of opinion has arisen, however, on the influence of sociology on marital choice. There is a common core of agreement on the initial importance of such variables as age, socioeconomic status, propinquity, race, previous marital status, and educational level, all of which tend to select homogamously. It is also apparent that these variables are not independent of each other, but tend to interact. Thus, propinquity may, in part, result from the fact that individuals with a similar cultural background tend to live close to each other (Eckland, 1968).

The division of opinion arises in regard to whether these cultural variables tend to serve as a screen for excluding candidates, or whether they actually are instrumental in the specific choice made. For sociologists like Kernodle (1959), Reiss (1960), and Coombs (1961), the cultural and social variables are not only important initially, but take precedence over individual and psychologically oriented variables, which are held to be only derivatives of the sociological conditions. Little weight is given to biological or genetic determinants or even idiosyncratic environmental influences.

An extreme case is that of Reiss (1960), who seems to discount completely the importance of individualistic need patterns when he says, "From our point of view, the love object could have been a number of people with similar socio-cultural characteristics. Chance factors led to it being this particular person. Thus, even here an 'individualistic' explanation is not needed" (p. 142).

That all sociologists do not really omit psychological factors from their theories of marital choice, however, is clearly evident in the "value" theory of Coombs (1961). He acknowledges the presence of individual differences in the socialization process in that "each person forms a somewhat unique system of values. Thus we may speak of both 'personal' and 'cultural' values" (Coombs, 1961, p. 51). In a study of matching on the basis of values (Coombs, 1966), Coombs found empirical support for his theory that value similarity is a positive factor for individuals who "date" each other. Such individuals were more likely to want to continue the relationship then those lacking value similarity.

The other position taken with regard to the role of sociological variables has been strongly championed by Robert F. Winch (1958). He acknowledges the initial importance of the aforementioned homogamous sociological variables, but denies that they determine marital choice. Rather, they define a field of eligibles from which the choice is made on the basis of unfulfilled personality needs. There are two types of needs.

Type I. The same need is gratified in both A and B but at very different levels of intensity. A negative interspousal correlation is hypothesized.

Type II: Different needs are gratified in A and B. The interspousal correlation may be hypothesized either to be positive or negative, contingent upon the pair of needs involved (Winch, 1958, pp. 94-95).

Winch's theory is, thus, essentially a two-stage one and his primary focus has been on the second stage of personality needs. To test his theory, he studied 25 married couples where one of the members was an undergraduate student at Northwestern University. The subjects were tested by means of a number of psychological tests, interviews, and case histories. The heart of the research lay in a series of personality needs adapted from Henry Murray for which the interviewers rated the subjects based on their performance during the "need-interview." The results generally supported the theory.

Winch's findings, however, have found little support among other researchers. He has been attacked by fellow sociologists (Bowman, 1955; Kernodle, 1959) for dabbling in areas where no self-respecting sociologist should tread (psychology and psychoanalysis). He has also (in their eyes) slighted the importance of sociological variables in determining marital choice by positing a successive-stage relationship between sociological and psychological variables rather than an interactional one in which the sociological variables serve as the determining factors and the psychological variables as the derivative factors.

Much of this criticism is petty and seems to imply that the search for knowledge must be made along prescribed lines within disciplines, and that *what* is found is not nearly so important as *who* found it. More serious criticism has come as a result of the empirical attempts of other researchers to verify Winch's findings.

Rossow (1957) found the theory vastly oversimplified, and Tharp (1963) criticized the methodology. The list of failures to replicate Winch's findings is rather large and only a sample need be mentioned (Schellenberg & Bee, 1960; Murstein, 1961; Heiss & Gordon, 1964).

Winch has made a spirited attack on the research findings contrary to his theory (1967). He has, nonetheless, admitted that some of the criticisms are valid and has not hesitated to modify his theory. He now favors an approach combining complementary needs with the satisfaction of role norms (see Bermann 1966). Where complementary need satisfaction is in accordance with the role norms for husbands and wives, the pairing of the man and woman should be highly stable. Where complementary needs and role norms are in conflict (e.g., a passive husband, domineering wife), greater difficulty should ensue.

Other research efforts have avoided the question of the order of importance of sociological and psychological determinants but have taken it for granted that both operate in some unspecified interaction. These efforts might be better termed approaches rather than theories, since none of them is sufficiently detailed or rigorously enough defined to be capable of empirical testing. Nonetheless, they do present other factors for consideration in understanding marital choice.

The importance of similarity in other than cultural, background variables has been emphasized by Burgess and Locke (1960). Reviewing the literature on marital choice, they found six factors to be influential: 1) propinquity; 2) group membership; 3) disapproval of marriage outside the ingroup; 4) concept of the ideal mate; 5) psychological similarity of prospective partner to one's parents; and 6) homogamy, or the tendency to marry another like the self. Their review of the literature suggests that the homogamy principle finds support in all of the aforementioned areas, but the authors did not put forth a clearcut theory accounting for these findings.

Another factor becoming increasingly the center of concern in interpersonal relationships is the relationship of the overall attractiveness of the individual to his ability to attract others. Boalt (1965) has incorporated this problem into his *summation* theory which he defines as follows:

> . . . in a sample of newly contracted marriages, husband and wife will be more or less evenly matched or each other's equals . . . every point on which one . . . is superior will tend to be associated with other points on which he is inferior, and vice versa. In other words, despite certain differences, husband and wife will prove to be very much on a par if all the circumstances are taken into consideration (p. 28).

He provides no data to test this assumption, but suggests a method of measurement for future research.

Recently, Cattell and Nesselroade (1967) suggested a variation of the egality or exchange approach described above. Their *completion* hypothesis

> . . . states that every person tends to seek in a partner much the same set of desirables—good looks, intelligence, emotional stability, etc.— but more so to the extent that he or she lacks them . . . [Thus] a marriage becomes viable because, as a team, it has the necessary qualities for adjustment and survival as a small group unit even though the members do not have them singly (p. 356).

The authors could present only a rather weak test of this hypothesis in their data and did not confirm it.

A significant advance in the problem of relating "cultural" and "psychological" variables occurred with the work of Kerckhoff and Davis (1962) and their presentation of a "filter" theory. Their data, derived from college couples, suggest that in the first stage of the relationship a couple choose each other on the basis of similarity of values, and that those who fail to agree break off the relationship. If, at this early stage, these short-term relationships are analyzed for psychological compatibility by comparing the expectations of one partner with the role which the other desires to play, no degree of compatibility above chance is found. If, however, couples who have been going together for a considerable amount of time are studied (longer than 18 months in the study), the *values* held prove to be no longer selective, but the *psychological-compatibility* principle takes over. Presumably, at this point, those with different values have broken off and the couples have had enough time to test their mutual expectations for a spouse and their partner's ability to fulfill them.

For nearly a decade this provocative study was unchallenged and unreplicated. Recently, however, a replication undertaken by Levinger, Senn, and Jorgensen (1970) has shattered the "tidiness" of the Kerckhoff and Davis findings. Using essentially the same measuring instruments and two large samples from the Universities of Colorado and Massachusetts, the authors failed to confirm any of the earlier findings. Their explanation is essentially twofold. Relationships among college youth have accelerated in development, and the Farber Index of Values and the Firo-B questionnaire, used earlier to measure value consensus and role compatibility respectively, are now seen as less appropriate. Also, the authors question whether a relationship leading to marriage, which is essentially a pairing commitment, can be successfully predicted from the responses to individual-centered measures.

In sum, whether pessimism or optimism is the correct reaction to earlier research depends on the point of view. That no viable theory has yet emerged may be a cause for pessimism. However, the increasing quality of research and the realization, apparent in recent research, that earlier theories have been overly simple and badly in need of replication, is a cause for optimism. Hopefully, newer research may profit from the willingness of earlier researchers to plod ahead with little earlier data or adequate measuring instruments to guide them.

The present theory to be offered does not pretend to encompass all the troublesome questions in this area. It does, however, seek to offer data and/or commentary on several perplexing questions which need further development if our knowledge of the determinants of marital choice is to be advanced. These questions include the following: 1) How do people get acquainted in the first place so that value similarity has a chance to operate? 2) Why should people like others who have similar values? 3) Do individuals marry those who are perceived as similar or do they sometimes marry perceived "opposites"? 4) Do all people succeed in marrying in accordance with their needs? 5) Do people marry on the basis of actual role-compatibility or *imagined* role-compatibility? 6) What is the role in marital choice of such variables as "self-esteem," "neuroticism," and "sexual drive?" 7) Are the perceptions and behavior of both men and women of equal importance in determining marital choice?

To attempt to answer these and other questions regarding marital choice, the author proposes to build on the pioneering efforts of earlier researchers by formulating a three-stage theory of marital choice called Stimulus-Value-Role (SVR). The three stages refer to the chronological sequence of the development of the relationship. Within each stage, the dynamics of interaction and attraction are explained in terms of social-exchange theory. The SVR theory will be described in detail, and data bearing on 19 hypotheses stemming from the theory will be briefly presented. The majority of the data stem from a four-year National Institute of Mental Health project investigating marital choice which was carried out mainly with college students in several New England colleges and universities. The main body of data came from two samples of 99 and 98 couples who were engaged or "going steady" and who were paid to take a series of tests and questionnaires. These included a revised form of the Edwards Personal Preference Schedule, the Marital Expectation Test devised by the author, and sexual behavior and background questionnaires.* A smaller group of 19 couples received intensive interviews, the Baughman modification of the Rorschach Inkblot Test, and a thematic test constructed by the author. Some of the results reported here have been described elsewhere in greater detail (Murstein 1967a; 1967b; 1971), but reference will also be made to portions of the author's data not as yet presented in published form.

---

* The Edwards Personal Preference Schedule used in the research was modified and reproduced by permission. Copyright 1953 by the Psychological Corporation, New York, New York. All rights reserved.

SVR THEORY

SVR theory holds that in a relatively "free choice" situation such as exists in the United States, most couples pass through three stages before deciding to marry. These stages will be defined and discussed in detail, but first the locus of the potential marital encounter merits some discussion.

"Open" and "Closed" Fields: An "open" field encounter refers to a situation in which the man and woman do not as yet know each other or have only a nodding acquaintance. Examples of such "open field" situations are "mixers," presence in a large school class at the beginning of the semester, and brief contacts in the office. The fact that the field is "open" indicates that either the man or the woman is free to start the relationship or to abstain from initiating it, as they wish. The contrary concept is the "closed field" situation in which both the man and woman are forced to interact by reason of the environmental setting in which they find themselves. Examples of such situations might be that of students in a small seminar in a college, members of a law firm, and workers in complementary professions such as doctor-nurse and boss-secretary. By interaction is meant contact through which the individual becomes acquainted with the nonstereotyped behavior of the "other," which is then evaluated according to the individual's own system of values. This system is a compendium of values acquired in the process of acculturalization to the traditional or current tastes of society, values acquired from one's peers and parents, values derived from experience, and those values resulting from genetically based predispositions which may be labeled "temperament."

Individuals may, of course, be attracted to members of the opposite sex without necessarily contemplating marriage. The fact that almost all persons in the United States eventually marry, however, suggests that many of the heterosexual social encounters of young adults contain at least the possibility of eventual marriage; consequently, the general heterosexual encounter has been treated as the first step toward possible marriage.

"Stimulus" Stage

In the "open field," an individual may be drawn to another based on his perception of the other's physical, social, mental, or reputational attributes and his perception of his own qualities that might be attractive to the other person. Because initial movement is due primarily to non-interactional cues not dependent on interpersonal interaction, these are categorized as "stimulus" values.

Qualities of Other

In the absence of other information, the attraction of the other will often depend on visual and auditory cues. The other may look beautiful, have a sexy voice, or may be "too old," "just right," or "too young." However, the attractiveness of the other person may be established even *prior* to the first meeting on the basis of information that he satisfies the system of values held by the perceiver. Furthermore, an individual may be viewed as physically unstimulating yet may possess compensating stimulus attributes. The rugged but ugly football tackle may attract a physically appealing woman because his stimulus impact as a virile, glamorous hero, as well as his promising financial prospects, may more than compensate for a forbidding physiognomy. Moreover, knowing that a man is a medical intern of a certain age and of the "right" religion may make him a desirable person for a woman to invite to a soirée.

In sum, in the first stage, perception of the other comprises the appreciation of all perceptions of the prospective partner, both sensate and nonsensate, which do not necessitate any kind of meaningful interaction. This stage is of crucial importance in the "open field," for, if the other person fails to provide sufficient reinforcement of one's value system at this stage, further contact is not sought. While the "prospect" in question might potentially be a highly desirable person with compatible values, the individual—foregoing opportunities for further contact—never finds this out. In consequence, it would appear that physically unattractive individuals are at a considerable handicap.

If marital choice depended only on the attractiveness of the other, we would have a largely unmarried population, since everyone would be drawn towards the relatively few highly attractive persons. The fact that the vast majority of persons do marry points out the necessity of considering at least two other factors: the person's own evaluation of how attractive he is to the other, and the conceptualization of marital choice as a kind of exchange-market phenomenon.

Perception of Self

As a function of his previous experiences, the individual builds up an image of himself in terms of his attractiveness to the opposite sex. If he sees himself as highly attractive, he is more likely to approach a highly attractive prospective partner than if he sees himself as unattractive. In actuality, we may suppose that each individual's self-concept covers a series of different aspects, and that a person might think of himself as adequate in some aspects and inadequate in others. There is some evidence, however (Kiesler & Baral, 1970), which suggests that even experiences which reduce self-esteem but which do not deal specifically with members of the opposite sex tend to influence subsequent "dating approaches" to the opposite sex.

Another factor to consider within the area of self-perception is the "fear of failure." Some individuals will avoid approaching attractive persons because they fear rejection, whereas others shrug off repeated rejections by a single person or different individuals without apparent damage to their self-esteem. The exact nature of the relationship between self-esteem and "fear of failure" remains to be clarified by future research, but it seems likely that both are highly important in determining approach behavior towards others.

Premarital Bargaining

Several writers have recently utilized some elementary economic concepts for explaining social behavior (Thibaut & Kelley, 1959; Homans, 1961; Blau, 1964). Essentially, these approaches maintain that each person tries to make social interaction as profitable as possible, *profit* being defined as the *rewards* he gains from the interaction minus the *costs* he must pay. By *rewards* are meant the pleasures, benefits, and gratifications an individual gains from a relationship. *Costs* are factors which inhibit or deter the performance of more preferred behaviors. A young man living in the Bronx, for example, might like a young lady from Brooklyn whom he met while both were at a resort. Back in the city, however, he may doubt that the rewards he might gain from the relationship would be worth the costs in time and fatigue of two-hour subway rides to Brooklyn.

Closely allied to rewards and costs are assets and liabilities. *Assets* are the commodities (behaviors or qualities) that the individual possesses which are capable of rewarding others and, in return, causing others to reciprocate by rewarding the individual. *Liabilities* are behaviors or qualities associated with an individual which are costly to others and thus, by reciprocity, costly also to the self.

A man who is physically unattractive (liability), for example, might desire a woman who has the asset of beauty. Assuming, however, that his nonphysical qualities are no more rewarding than hers, she gains less profit than he does from the relationship and thus his suit is likely to be rejected. Rejection is a cost to him because it may lower his self-esteem and increase his fear of failure in future encounters; hence, he may decide to avoid courting women whom he perceives as much above him in attractiveness.

Contrariwise, he is likely to feel highly confident of success if he tries to date a woman even less attractive than himself where he risks little chance of rejection (low cost). However, the reward value of such a conquest is quite low, so that the profitability of such a move is also low. As a consequence, an experienced individual is likely to express a maximum degree of effort and also obtain the greatest reward at the least cost when he directs his efforts at someone of approximately equal physical attraction, assuming all other variables are constant.

During the first moments of contact, the individual may attempt to supplement his visual impression of the other with information regarding the other's role in society, professional aspirations, and background. Persons attracted to each other, thus, are likely to be balanced for the total weighted amalgam of stimulus characteristics even though, for a given trait, gross disparities may exist. Men, for example, tend to weight physical attractiveness in a partner more than women do, whereas women give greater weight to professional aspiration in the partner; accordingly, although physical attraction may play a leading role, it is hypothesized that the weighted pool of stimulus attractions that each possesses for the other will be approximately equal if individuals are to progress into the second stage of courtship.

Because the author's research couples were largely in an advanced state of courtship at the time of testing, it was impossible to directly test this hypothesis. However, it was possible to test certain consequences of successful passage through the "stimulus" stage. Focusing on one of the most important of the stimulus attributes which should be relatively unchanged by the brief passage of time in courtship (physical attraction), the following prediction was made:

Hypothesis 1. *As a result of "bargaining," premarital couples will show greater than chance similarity with respect to physical attraction, whether objectively or subjectively measured.*

In a study by the present author on 99 college couples who were either engaged or going steady, the discrepancy in physical attractiveness of actual couples, as derived from judgments of photos of the couples, was significantly smaller than those of the same persons randomly matched $(p < .01)$. The discrepancy in perception of the boyfriend (girlfriend) by the real couples was not significantly different from that of the contrived couples, but a strong trend toward significance was found with respect to the discrepancy in self-evaluations of attractiveness $(p = .06)$.

In a second study on 98 couples, no photos were taken, but the discrepancy of self-judgments of attractiveness in actual couples proved to be significantly smaller $(p < .01)$ than in contrived couples. However, again, no significant difference was found between the discrepancies in perception of the partner's physical attractiveness by the members of real couples and those of the artificial couples. Considering the select and restricted range of our sample and also the fact that we have focused on only one of the stimulus variables without considering the possibly compensating effects of the other stimulus variables, it can be concluded that the stimulus portion of SVR theory appears to be substantiated.

Other support for bargaining or exchange within the "stimulus" stage may be derived from a number of studies. Carter and Glick (1970), working with demographic data from the 1960 census, showed that "A Negro who marries a white person tends to have superior qualities (specifically, a higher educational level) as compared with a Negro who marries another Negro; . . . a white person who marries a Negro tends to have inferior qualities (educational level) as compared with a white person who marries another white person" [p. 127].

In the same context, there is evidence for a relationship between lightness of skin, color and mobility among Negro women (Warner, Junker & Adams, 1941; Udry & Bauman, 1968). If one assumes that Negroes occupy an inferior status position in society compared to Caucasians, hardly a startling assumption, these results conform well to an exchange paradigm.

Turning to physical appearance, Illsley (1955; cited in Lipset and Bendix, 1959) reported that lower-status women who married higher-status men tended to be both taller and healthier than their non-mobile counterparts. Holmes and Hatch (1938) likewise reported a correlation between beauty and probability of marriage in an era when, for a woman, marriage was clearly superior in status to singleness. Last, Elder (1969) found that the tendency of a man's social rank to exceed his wife's pre-marital rank was related to her physical attractiveness. Where a woman had more education than her husband, however, she was more likely to come from a physically unattractive group than a physically attractive group. Here too, therefore, strong support is found for the exchange principle within the "stimulus" stage of courtship.

"Value" Stage

Assume for the moment that mutual "stimulus" attraction has occurred between a young man and woman at a "mixer" dance, and that they sit down and talk to each other. They are now entering the second stage, that of "value comparison." Unlike the "stimulus" stage in which attributes of the partner are evaluated without any necessary interpersonal contact, the value comparison stage involves the appraisal of value compatibility through verbal interaction. The kinds of values explored through discussion are apt to be much more varied than those possible in the "stimulus" stage. The couple may compare their attitudes towards life, politics, religion, sex, and the roles of men and women in society and marriage. The fact that the couple is now interacting also permits more continuous and closer scrutiny of physical appearance, as well as other important factors such as temperament, "style" of perceiving the world, and ability to relate to others.

It is possible that closer appraisal of physical qualities and temperament will lead to a changed opinion regarding the desirability of the partner, and this may result in an attempt to terminate the contact as soon as gracefully possible. If contact has been made on the basis of strong stimulus attraction, however, it is more likely that the couple will remain in the second stage, continuing to assess the compatibility of their values.

Should the couple find that they hold similar value orientations in important areas, they are apt to develop much stronger positive feelings for each other than they experienced in the "stimulus" stage. One reason for this is that when an individual encounters another who holds similar values, he gains support for the conclusion that his own values are correct; his views are given social validation (Berscheid & Walster, 1969). Further, many values are intensely personal and are so linked to the self-concept that rejection of these values is experienced as rejection of the self and acceptance of them implies validation of the self. Providing we have a reasonably positive self-image, we tend to be attracted to those persons whom we perceive as validating it. Also, perceived similarity of values may lead to the assumption that the other likes us, and there is empirical evidence that we like those individuals whom we think like us (Berscheid & Walster, 1969).

Last, we may note that persons who have similar values are likely to engage in similar activities and thus reward each other by validating each other's commitment to the activity. Moreover, because these activities are similar, they are apt to have similar reward value in the world at large, thus further drawing the couple together since they share equal status in their milieu. We have already indicated that individuals of equal standing in attractiveness are most apt to be drawn to each other because of their equal ability to reward each other. In sum, the holding of similar values should be a major factor in drawing two individuals together. Our second hypothesis, therefore, is:

Hypothesis 2. *Individuals considering marriage tend to show greater than chance similarity with regard to their hierarchy of values concerning marriage.*

In a study by the present author, a group of 99 engaged or "going steady" couples showed a greater correlation for the ranking of 10 values relating to marriage than did randomly matched couples. In another study by the present author, 19 engaged or "going steady" couples were intensively interviewed and were given a series of "depth" personality tests and a number of questionnaires. The data were used as a basis for formulating a Q sort of 100 statements referring to personality, temperament, and values. Of the eight items which referred to values, actual couples showed significantly less discrepancy than artificially contrived couples for six variables: "conventionality," "conservatism," "importance of physical attractiveness in others," "moralistic," "concerned with philosophical problems," and "committed to intellectual activities." No variables dealing with values were found to be significantly more discrepant for actual than for contrived couples, thus strongly confirming the hypothesis that marital choice is dependent on value similarity.

Returning to our hypothetical couple, it would logically follow that, if the encounter proves mutually satisfactory, attempts may be made to extend and continue the relationship on future occasions. The participants decide that they like each other. The overall decision of whether to continue to view the relationship as possibly leading to marriage will probably depend upon the summative effects of value congruence with respect to the values leading to the encounter and the values encountered in verbal interaction. A beautiful woman, for example, may be desirable even if her values depart somewhat from those of the man. Conversely, an unusually strong satisfaction derived from similarly held values may offset the fact that the physical appearance of the partner is only minimally satisfying.

It is possible that the people may decide to marry on the basis of stimulus attraction and verbalized value similarity. However, for most persons, these are necessary but not sufficient conditions for marriage. It is also important that the couple be able to *function* in compatible roles. By *role* is meant "the behavior that is characteristic and expected of the occupant of a defined position in [a] group" (English & English, 1958, p. 468). A role is thus a norm for a particular relationship and for particular situations. The role of husband, for example, may be perceived by the wife as embodying tenderness and acceptance of her. This role, however, does not necessarily clash with another role of the husband, that of ability to aggressively maintain the economic security of the family. There are, in short, a multiplicity of roles for the different kinds of situations that one encounters.

In the premarital phase, however, the partner's ability to function in the desired role is not as readily observable as his verbalized expression of views on religion, economics, politics, and how men should treat women. Knowing, for example, how much emotional support the partner will give when the individual fails a history examination presupposes an advanced stage of intimacy. It is for this reason that the "role" stage is placed last in the time sequence leading to marital choice.

"Role" Stage

There are many tasks which face the couple in the "role" stage before they move into marriage. Rapoport (1963) has listed nine of these, but the limitations of the type of data collected by the present author as well as a somewhat different conceptual framework dictate limiting the analysis to three broad areas: perceived role "fit," personal adequacy, and sexual compatibility.

Concerning role "fit," it may be noted that, as the couple relationship ripens, the members increasingly confide in each other and thus become aware of a broader range of each other's behavior than heretofore. They may also become more cognizant of what they desire in a future spouse, and more consciously compare these expectations with their perception of the partner. They also become increasingly aware of the impact that their own behavior has on the partner and whether he considers these behaviors to be appropriate. Mutual role "fit" should be mutually rewarding and result in a desire to assure the continuity of satisfaction by putting the relationship on a more or less permanent basis through marriage.

A second task is to take the measure of one's own personal adequacy and that of the partner since, for example, moodiness, inability to make decisions, dislike of the self, and neuroticism may be high costs to bear in marriage. The third task involves the necessity of attaining sexual compatibility whether by achieving a good sexual relationship in practice or by agreement as to the degree of sexuality which will be expressed during the "role" stage prior to marriage. Throughout the three areas, it will be seen that the roles of men and women are not only often dissimilar, but often of unequal importance to courtship progress (henceforth called CP). Before considering these three areas, however, the utilization of a formal criterion of the progress of the relationship in the "role" stage will be described.

CP as a Measure of Progress in the Relationship

Because most of our couples had known each other at least six months and often longer at the time of initial testing, it could be assumed that they were in the "role" stage of the relationship. To measure progress in this stage a longitudinal measure of the strength of the relationship based on the earlier work of Kerckhoff and Davis (1962) was employed.

Six months after the initial testing of each of our samples of 99 and 98 couples, respectively, a questionnaire was mailed to each participant to determine whether each individual believed that the relationship had progressed, remained stationary, or regressed in the interim. The average of the two scores of each couple (4 point scale in the first study, 5 point scale in the second one) constituted the measure of the couple's CP. These follow-up scores were obtained from over 95 per cent of the initially tested couples.

Role "Fit"

Is the Partner Perceived to be Similar or Opposite to the Self?

We have noted earlier that research on marital choice has offered luke-warm support to the homogamy principle and even less support to the principle of complementary needs. SVR theory, as described so far, has been in accord with the homogamy principle with respect to the "stimulus" and "value" stages. Role similarity, however, is not necessarily advantageous during the "role" stage of courtship. The explanation for the lack of usefulness of role-homogamy lies in a basic distinction between values and roles.

Values are experienced by most persons as part and parcel of the "self," whereas roles, although they may serve as goals, are often *means* to goals. Should the goals change, therefore, the roles may also change. The wife may play the role of the loving homemaker so long as she enjoys the rewards of appreciation and affection from her spouse. If she learns that her husband is about to divorce her, however, she may exchange this role for that of "the woman scorned." Since roles are often behavioral means to an end, it is possible that, in some instances, role-similarity may impede the goals of one or both partners. Suppose that both husband and wife desire to essay the role of homemaker and neither wishes to enter the business world. The result is no family income. It is clear, therefore, that what is important is the compatibility of roles with goals, not whether roles are homogamous or complementary.

An individual's ideal-self may be termed a goal more than a role since it is an end he strives towards rather than a part he actually plays. In similar vein, the goal he sets for his partner is embodied in his concept of ideal-spouse. The extent to which an individual is currently able to meet his personal goals is measured by his self-ideal-self discrepancy, and the perceived fulfillment of his expectation for his partner is determined by the discrepancy between his perception of partner and his concept of ideal-spouse.

To understand why role satisfaction for some individuals is associated with perceived similarity of self to the partner while for others it involves perceived dissimilarity, we must consider four perceptual concepts: self, ideal-self, perceived partner, and ideal-spouse. Consider first the relationship of the concept of ideal-spouse to ideal-self. It is to be expected that these variables should be highly correlated because idealized expectations in marriage are generally similar for most of the individuals within the same culture.

The perception of the partner should also be relatively highly correlated with the perceptions of both ideal-spouse and ideal-self in a society such as ours which emphasizes free choice. The "dating" structure, after all, encourages "shopping around" until some tangible approximation of the ideal is discovered. The slightly lower expected correlations of the perceived partner with ideal-self and with ideal-spouse, compared to the ideal-spouse, ideal-self correlation, should merely reflect the fact that the partner, no matter how strongly admired, never quite reaches the ideal. In any event, we should expect that the perceptions of partner, ideal-self, and ideal-spouse, should be highly correlated with one another. Whether or not the partner is really as similar to the ideal-self and ideal-spouse as the subject believes he is, is a question that we shall deal with later.

Focusing on the question of perceived similarity to the partner, it is proposed that, if the individual is highly satisfied with himself as determined by a high correlation between the self and ideal-self, and, if it is true, as has been earlier proposed, that the concepts of ideal-self, ideal-spouse, and perceived partner are highly intercorrelated, then it follows that the individual will attempt to marry someone whom he perceives as highly similar to himself.

If, however, the subject is highly dissatisfied with himself (low self, ideal-self correlation), he will still want to marry someone close to his ideal-self and ideal-spouse since, as noted earlier, these variables are largely determined by stereotyped normative value acquired in the process of culturalization. The difference between high and low self-acceptance persons with respect to these aforementioned variables, therefore, would not be expected to be very large; accordingly, the fact that the self is unlike the ideal-self will also result in the self being unlike the ideal-spouse and perceived partner. To the extent that the low self-acceptance person succeeds in meeting a reasonable facsimile of his ideal-spouse, therefore, he will tend to perceive that person as less similar to himself than would be the case for the high self-acceptance person. The perception of the partner as relatively similar or dissimilar to the self is, thus, largely a derivative of the position of the self with respect to the trinity of desiderata, the ideal-self, ideal-spouse, and perceived partner. Figure 1 illustrates this state of affairs graphically with the correlation between concepts represented by the inverse of the physical distance between them. Our formal hypothesis for this event is as follows:

Hypothesis 3. *Couples with high-acceptance (HSA) view their partner as significantly more similar to themselves than couples with low self-acceptance (LSA).*

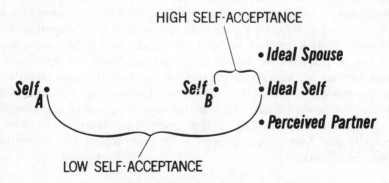

FIG. 1. *A, whose self and ideal-self concepts are far apart (low self-acceptance), will also see partner as unlike him, whereas B, whose self and ideal-self are close together (high self-acceptance), will also see partner as highly similar to the self.*

In the author's sample of 99 couples (Murstein, 1971), the 33 men with the highest self, ideal-self correlations on the author's Marriage Expectation Test were considered to be HSA men, while the 33 men with the lowest self, ideal-self correlations were labeled LSA men. The HSA men showed a correlation of .73 between the self and the perceived girl-friend, whereas LSA men showed a correlation of .35, the difference being highly significant $(p. < .01)$. For HSA and LSA women, the correlations were .55 and .30, respectively, the correlations again differing significantly $(p < .01)$. Thus, the results of both male and female samples strongly support Hypothesis 3. These data indicate that satisfaction with the self leads to a tendency to choose partners perceived as generally similar to the self, and this tendency is diminished for those persons dissatisfield with themselves.

The fact that even the LSA subjects showed a positive correlation for self and partner is most probably due to the fact that our LSA subjects are only relatively low in self-acceptance. The correlations of LSA subjects between self and ideal-self (.65 for women; .69 for men) may mean that persons volunteering for an extensive study on marital choice generally tend to be quite satisfied with themselves. The second factor contributing to a positive self-partner correlation is that certain items are viewed similarly by most persons of a similar economic status and educational level. Since economic status and educational level are selective for marriage, a certain degree of positive correlation should be found in all items which are not culture-free.

It is not difficult to illustrate that the concepts of homogamy or complementarity, considered without regard to role compatibility, are not very meaningful. Suppose that a man and woman each view themselves as ambitious. If he desires an ideal-spouse who would be low in ambition, but he perceives his partner to be very ambitious, the result will be homogamy of self-characteristics but low perceived role-compatibility. She, on the other hand, may desire an ambitious spouse and, if she perceives her male partner this way, we have an example of homogamy of self-characteristics leading to high role-compatibility. Thus, complementarity and homogamy are seen as inconsequential for determining role-compatibility.

Perceptual Congruency, Perceptual Accuracy, and Courtship Progress

The more "A" likes "B," the more he discloses his private world to "B." In a "dating" situation, such a disclosure is rewarding to "B" because it marks him as worthy of receiving intimate information and, accordingly, raises his self-esteem. Moreover, the receipt of intimate information from "A" encourages "B" to reciprocate by offering information at equal levels of intimacy. This theoretical sequence of events has recently received solid empirical verification in the work of Worthy, Gary, and Kahn (1969).

Once engaged in mutual disclosures, the tendency is for couples to proceed to continuously more intimate cycles of rewarding disclosure. The act of disclosure is not only rewarding to the listener, but may serve as a cathartic agent for the discloser who himself gains a feeling of acceptance and other rewards from the attention of the other. Individuals who attain ever deeper levels of mutual disclosure, therefore, should make good CP, whereas those who do not reach these levels are more apt to flounder in their courtship.

In addition, the level of disclosure reached should have a profound effect on the perception of the partner and on the individual's own perceptual world. Because they have attained deeper levels of disclosure, couples destined to make good CP should become more accurate in predicting each other's self and ideal-self concepts. Also, because disclosure to a friend usually meets acceptance, it increases liking by the discloser; hence, couples reaching an intimate level of disclosure should manifest considerable perceptual congruence between their concept of ideal-spouse and their perception of their partner. The following two predictions were made therefore:

Hypothesis 4. *Couples who show good CP were able to make more accurate predictions of the partner's self and ideal-self at the beginning of the study (six months earlier) than were poor CP couples.*

Women making good CP tended to have estimated more accurately how their boyfriends saw their ideal selves ($p < .01$) and actual selves ($p < .05$) than did poor CP women. Similarly, men making good CP were more accurate than low CP men in estimating their girlfriends' ideal-selves ($p < .01$), though only a trend was noted for estimating the girlfriends' selves.

Hypothesis 5. *Couples who make good CP showed greater compatibility between their conception of ideal-spouse and their perception of the partner than couples making poor CP.*

In the author's study of 99 couples, members of couples who subsequently in six months time made good CP showed significantly less discrepancy ($p < .05$) between perception of the partner and the ideal-spouse desired than did members of poor CP couples; hence, Hypotheses 4 and 5 are strongly confirmed.

Intra- and Interperceptual Compatibility

From an objective viewpoint, it might be rather difficult for individuals to judge adequately whether their partners would make good spouses. Relatively few persons play the role of husband and wife before they are married. Even those persons who live together cannot be said to be completely or even adequately duplicating the marital role, because a) each is relatively free to sunder the arrangement with little or no societal disapproval, and b) the couple does not usually play the role of husband and wife with respect to interactions with the outside world.

The average couple in courtship have seen each other not only for a relatively limited amount of time, but also within only a limited number of roles. In addition, courtship elicits from individuals the most socially desirable conduct which, unfortunately, may not be typical of their usual repertoire of behaviors. If couples do not really know each other, but, in accordance with the dictates of society, feel they must be "in love," it follows that a) the congruence of their perception of their ideal-spouse and partner must be quite high and b) if the actual self-concept of one partner and the ideal-spouse desired by the other individual are compared, the congruence would be expected to be relatively low.*

From a reward-exchange viewpoint, the origin of liking may be presumed to lie in the similar perceptual outlook of the couple, with the reciprocal rewards this entails. However, although perceived similarity of outlook may lead initially to liking, once individuals are committed to each other, it is the liking that may very well influence the perception (Newcomb, 1961) ; thus, as we like the other more and more, we perceive him as behaving more and more in accordance with our needs and wishes. If the data for how the partner actually behaves is sparse or absent, we *imagine* that he would behave as we would like him to, nonetheless, because this assumption is necessary to justify our increased commitment to him; thus imagined role-compatibility should greatly exceed actual role-compatibility.

---

* It is only fair to note that part of the difference between the first correlation described above (Self$_M$, Ideal-Spouse$_M$) and the second one (Self$_W$, Ideal-Spouse$_M$) lies in the fact that the first correlation is an intraperceptual one in which both perceptions stem from the same person (man), whereas the second correlation is interperceptual in that it compares the percepts of two different persons; hence, the first correlation should be more reliable since repeated measurements stemming from the same person tend to have less error variance than is the case where percepts stem from two different sources. However, in actual research, the enormity of the difference between the size of the two correlations in favor of the intraperceptual one makes it highly unlikely that differences in reliability alone could account for this fact.

Hypothesis 6. *Perceived compatibility as derived from intraperceptions (perceptions stemming from the same person) is significantly greater than compatibility as derived from interperceptions (perceptions stemming from both members of the couple).*

In the author's study of 99 couples (Murstein, 1967a), the intraperceptual correlations of ideal-spouse desired by a subject and his perception of his boyfriend (girlfriend) were .63 for women and .69 for men. The correlations for role satisfaction when ideal-spouse desired by one partner was compared with the self of the other were .20 for $self_M$, ideal spouse$_W$, and .17 for $self_W$, ideal-spouse$_M$. The differences between intra- and interperceptions are clearly significant in both cases ($p < .01$) and in accordance with the hypothesis. In view of the clear support given to Hypotheses 3, 4, 5, and 6, it may be concluded that role "fit" seems to be an important factor in the "role" stage of courtship.

Personality Adequacy

An individual's self-acceptance and neuroticism determine his attractiveness to his partner for several reasons. First, there is less cost in relating to a nonneurotic, HSA person than to an inadequate, LSA one because the former makes fewer unreasonable demands on the relationship, and his demands, when made, are apt to be more logical and easily satisfied. Also, such an individual is more apt to come closer to the model of the ideal-spouse and to have social stimulus value in the eyes of others.

In a study on friendship which seems applicable here, Kipnis (1961) has pointed out yet another function of interpersonal relationships. She found that an individual begins a friendship (and by extension I apply her results to courtship as well) so that his self-esteem may rise as a consequence of the new relationship. To the extent that the relationship does not yield this reward, there is a considerable probability that the friendship will be terminated.

If personal adequacy is an asset, however, it seems logical that highly adequate individuals will not be satisfied with persons less adequate than themselves because of the higher cost of relating to them, and because rewards in terms of possible gains in self-acceptance are likely to be smaller. They will, therefore, tend to reject these individuals at such time as the disparity in adequacy becomes manifest. The result is that couples who progress to the stage of serious courtship may be expected to have similar self-acceptance and neuroticism scores. Given the occurrence of occasional mismatchings, it could be predicted that, with the passage of time, individuals who differ widely in personal adequacy are more likely to experience disparate degrees of profit from the relationship. They are more likely to break up, therefore, than are those with similar degrees of adequacy. We may, therefore, formulate the following three hypotheses:

Hypothesis 7. *Individuals tend to choose partners whose level of self-acceptance is similar to their own.*

In the study of 99 couples described earlier (Murstein, 1971), the self-acceptance levels (self, ideal-self *r*) of the girlfriends of HSA men were compared with the self-acceptance levels of the girlfriends of LSA men. The respective correlations were .86 and .65, respectively, the difference being significant ($p < .01$). Further, the self-acceptance of the boyfriends of HSA women was significantly higher ($r = .85$) than that of boyfriends of LSA women ($r = .69$), the difference being significant at the .01 level. Thus, Hypothesis 7 is strongly confirmed.

Hypothesis 8. *Individuals tend to choose partners whose level of neuroticism is similar to their own.*

In the study of 99 couples by the present author (Murstein, 1967b), all subjects had taken the Minnesota Multiphasic Personality Inventory (MMPI). The 198 profile sheets of the men and women were given to a clinician having some familiarity with the MMPI.* Knowing only the profile scores and sex of the subjects, he was asked to sort the sheets into three piles: those with no problems of emotional adjustment, those with slight problems, and those with evidence of considerable disturbance. From his sorting of protocols, the expectancy of a couple falling in the same category by chance was computed and found to be 51 per cent. The actual percentage of time a couple was placed in the same category was 59 and the difference proved to be significant ($p < .03$). An attempt to use a more formal approach was made by correlating, for the couples, the sum of the three scales of the MMPI which make up what is popularly referred to as the Neurotic Triad. The obtained correlation of .10, although in the predicted direction, failed to achieve significance.

Studies by other researchers such as Pond, Ryle, and Hamilton (1963), Slater (1946), Willoughby (1936), and Richardson (1939) found significant relationships between neuroticism in marital partners, but these reports, unlike the present study, were unable to demonstrate that the neuroticism was present before the onset of marriage. In sum, the evidence shows slight support for the hypothesis. It is believed, however, that the selective nature of our sample may have restricted the range of

---

* I am indebted to Professor Philip A. Goldberg, who served as the judge for the sorting.

the correlation coefficient and that a more representative population would yield stronger evidence of a positive correlation of neuroticism between couples.

Hypothesis 9. *Individuals are more likely to make good CP when they are going with a partner of comparable neuroticism than when they are courting a person with a dissimilar degree of neuroticism.*

In a study by the author (Murstein, 1967b), the correlation between couples on the "neurotic triad" of the MMPI making good CP six months after the administration of the MMPI was .33, whereas for those making poor CP it was −.53. The difference between these coefficients is quite highly significant $(p < .01)$ and substantiates the hypothesis.

Choosing as Opposed to "Settling" for a Partner

One sometimes gains the impression from the literature on marital choice that everyone sets out to seek a partner who can fulfill one's personal needs, and that somehow or other each individual more or less manages to find a partner admirably or maliciously suited for himself; hence, some psychiatrists (Kubie, 1956; Mittelman, 1944) assume that even neurotics seek each other out. From the conception expressed here that "personal adequacy" is attractive both because of its high reward value and low cost, a rather different conclusion is reached. Individuals possessing the greatest number of assets and the fewest liabilities should be able to choose partners appropriately suited to them with a greater probability of success than those who are quite low in marital assets and high in liabilities; consequently, despite the rationalizing process which would tend to force an individual to view his prospective spouse as close to his heart's desire, it is predicted that LSA and/or neurotic persons, for example, should experience less satisfaction with their "steady" or fiancé (e) than HSA and/or nonneurotic persons.* Whereas HSA persons "choose" each other because each represents the potential for profitable experiences for the other, LSA persons are more apt to "settle" for each other for want of a better alternative.

Hypothesis 10. *HSA individuals are more likely to perceive their partners as approaching their concept of ideal-spouse than are LSA individuals.*

In the author's study of 99 couples, the correlation for HSA men between perception of the ideal-spouse and girlfriend on the Marital

---

* My research data show that these two variables are moderately correlated $(r = .57;$ reliability of measures was between .80 and .90).

Expectation Test was .88, whereas for the LSA men it was .70, a highly significant difference $(p < .01)$. For HSA and LSA women, the respective correlations were .86 and .69. These correlations were also significantly different $(p < .01)$, thus strongly confirming the hypothesis.

Other evidence supporting the concept of self-esteem (which appears closely allied to that of self-acceptance) as an important variable in the study of interpersonal attraction comes from Walster (1965) and from Kiesler and Baral (1970). The former found that female subjects undergoing an experience which enhanced their self-esteem were more likely to reject the advances of a male research assistant than were subjects who were made to experience a reduction in their self-esteem.

Kiesler and Baral found that male subjects experiencing a treatment designed to enhance self-esteem were more likely to approach an attractive female confederate for a "date" than were men who received a self-esteem defeating experience. On the other hand, the low self-esteem men were more likely than the high-esteem men to approach a less attractive female confederate. The above studies are consistent with the thesis that low self-esteem persons are less selective and aim lower in their interpersonal choices than do high self-esteem individuals. The support for the "personal adequacy" hypotheses also indicates that it is a key factor in marital choice.

Sex-Drive

Although much attention has been given to the concepts of role and value in the literature on marital choice, there has been little concern with drives and in particular, the sex-drive. Drive is defined here as "A tendency initiated by shifts in physiological [or psychological] balance to be sensitive to stimuli of a certain class and to respond in any of a variety of ways that are related to the attainment of a certain goal" (English & English, 1958, pp. 163-164). Drives function in a similar manner to values in that, for a given drive, the more similar the intensity of that drive for each member of the couple, the more compatible the couple. The reason why similarity of sex-drive is rewarding is that it leads to a similar desire for frequency of sexual contacts and an optimum ratio of desire for sex compared to participation in sex.

Hypothesis 11. *Couples going together exhibit a greater than chance similarity of sexual drive level.*

The author's sample of 99 couples (Murstein, 1970a) received a sex-questionnaire which asked four questions: recency of last orgasm, average weekly frequency of orgasm, strength of self-perceived sex-drive, and difficulty in control of sex-drive. Actual couples tended to be significantly less discrepant than randomly matched couples with respect to recency of orgasm ($p < .01$) and strength of self-perceived sex drive ($p < .01$). These data are consistent with the perception of sexual drive as a homogamous selective variable in marital choice.

There are, however, special considerations attached to the sex-drive variable which merit further discussion. It should be noted first that research indicates that the sex-drive of men is in general stronger than that of woman, when sex-drive is defined as the consciously experienced desire for relief from sexual tension through sexual activity (Burgess & Wallin, 1953; Terman, 1938; Kinsey et al., 1953; Shuttleworth, 1959). Men experience a greater number of orgasms over a weekly period and are more easily aroused by a wide variety of stimuli which fail to arouse women to an equal pitch. Moreover, men appear to be sensitive to the tension of accumulated semen which serves as a continuing pressure to obtain sexual release, whereas no comparable mechanism seems to be operating in women.

Conversely, the sex-drive of women seems to be more sensitive to learning patterns, and the latter vary more with the demands of the interpersonal situation than is the case for men; thus Kinsey's data indicate that marriage elevates the sexual orgasm frequency of men only 63 per cent, whereas it elevates that of women 560 per cent (Shuttleworth, 1959). The less flexible nature of the male sex-drive should make the discrepancy between masculine and feminine drive more of a problem for the man, since his need for a more constant outlet is greater than that of the woman. Further, a man with a low sex-drive, because of the difference in sex-drive between the sexes, is more likely than the high sex-drive man to approximate the sex-drive of his girlfriend. It follows, therefore, that it is the high sex-drive man who is likely to experience the greatest sexual frustration in the relationship.

It is clear from the mass of literature relating to sex, however, that the implications of differences in sex-drive are rarely restricted to the sexual area. Instead, they are likely to strongly influence the perception of the other person's personality and commitment to the relationship. The stereotyped response of the low sex-drive woman to the insistence of the high sex-drive male partner for frequent intercourse is "You are just using me for my body." The high sex-drive male may perceive his partner, however, as "cold" or indifferent. It is also possible that the satisfaction of his more imperious sexual needs may result in less sensitivity to the psychological needs of his partner and less concern over the extent of the couple's compatibility regarding personality needs. The result should be that couples in which the man possesses a high sex-drive should be less likely to perceive their partner as meeting their criterion of ideal-spouse than would be the case for low sex-drive men. Also, these couples should, in general, be less accurate in their estimates of the perceptions of the partner. In short, couples in which the man possesses a high sex-drive are less likely to make good CP than couples in which the man has a low sex-drive.

Woman's sexuality, however, being more dependent on the interpersonal relationship between her and her partner, should not follow the same pattern. Rather, women with good interpersonal relationships (good CP) should, as a *result,* experience a higher rate of orgasm than women with poor CP. High and low sex-drive women should not differ, however, in the accuracy of their perceptions of their partner because the sex-drive for women, being more a resultant of the relationship and being less dependent on hormonal influence, does not serve as a disruptive drive. The following two hypotheses are therefore advanced:

Hypothesis 12. *Couples in which the male sex-drive is high will show less role-compatibility and less CP than couples in which the male sex-drive is low. Women making good CP will, however, manifest a higher average orgasm-rate than poor CP women.*

For a sample of 99 men, various role-compatibility discrepancies were compared for men above and below the median of response to each of the four sex questions described in Hypothesis 11. Of a total of 40 tests run, eight were significant at the .05 level or beyond. The data indicated that men with sex-drives below the median were seen as more closely approximating the ideal-spouse desired by their partner and tended to so perceive themselves. Further, these men perceived their own partners as more closely approximating their own ideal-spouse. In addition, a trend ($p < .10$) was found for low self-perceived sex-drive for men to be associated with good CP. A second study with a new sample of 98 couples, indicated that the 25 men with the lowest weekly average orgasm rates made significantly better CP ($p < .01$) than the 25 men with the highest rate. The earlier significance of self-perceived sex-drive, however, was not confirmed. Women making good CP did not manifest a higher average orgasm-rate than poor CP women in the first study, but did so in the second one ($p < .01$) when the top and bottom thirds of the sample were compared instead of the two halves. The results, while not completely consistent, generally confirm the association between sex-drive and role-compatibility, and between sex-drive and CP.

Hypothesis 13. *Men with high sex-drives are significantly less accurate in their estimate of how their partners perceive them, and how their partners perceive themselves, than are low sex-drive men.*

In the study on 98 couples, the author found that low sex-drive men were significantly more accurate in estimating how their girlfriends perceived them and how their girlfriends perceived themselves than high sex-drive men. Similarly, the girlfriends of low sex-drive men could more accurately predict the ideal-selves of their boyfriends, their boyfriends' self-images, and how their boyfriends perceived them. The data from Hypotheses 11, 12, and 13 thus confirm the facilitative effects of homogamy of sex-drive on the relationship of a couple, and the disruptive effects of the high sex-drive of the man.

The Greater Importance of the Man in Courtship

From the dawn of recorded time, men have manifested greater control over their partner's behavior than have women. In the United States, even as late as the nineteenth century, men had the power to deny women full legal status, political franchise, and equal economic opportunity (Murstein, 1970b). Currently, most of these inequities have been greatly reduced, but it is nevertheless true that economic and social power is still disproportionately distributed by sex, with the average woman still less powerful than the average man.

From the point of view of our marital bargaining model, the effect is that the cost of abstaining from marriage is greater for women than for men. The status of the unmarried woman is lower than that of the unmarried man, and her economic skills are apt to be inferior and hence less rewarded in the market. To compound the difficulty for women, the age difference between marriageable men and women, the women's shorter age range of marriageability, and their longer life-span put them in greater supply and in less demand than men. The effect of this greater power of men is that, in courting situations, the man is

. . . the one who usually takes the most active role. He often is the one who actively initiates the relationship by asking for a date. He also is more often the one who is the first to commit himself to the relationship and who, in the everyday aspects of the courtship, decides about such activities as dinner arrangements, movies, and dances. The woman occupies the more passive role as the recipient of the man's wooing. She is not as likely to manifest signs of disturbance during the courtship simply because she has less role-prescribed need to initiate the contact and to make decisions. . . . If she accepts the man as a legitimate suitor, he is expected to shoulder most of the interpersonal responsibilities from that point on (Murstein, 1967b:450).

The result is that, although the greatest likelihood of good CP occurs when both members of a couple possess the same degree of neuroticism, the impact of neuroticism for the relationship when only one member is neurotic should be greater when the neurotic partner is the man.

Hypothesis 14. *Courtship progress is impaired more by neuroticism in the man than by neuroticism in the woman.*

The author's data on neuroticism (Murstein 1967b) substantiated this hypothesis in that the CP of his 99 couples was associated significantly with the mental health of the man ($p < .01$) but not with that of the woman.

Because the man's power in marital choice is greater than that of his partner, confirmation by the woman of his self and ideal-self concepts should have greater consequences for CP than confirmation of the woman's self and ideal-self concepts. The man's tendency to reinforce the woman's self and ideal-self image should make her like him a great deal but should not affect CP as much as in the former case, because it is the man who usually proposes. Moreover, since the initial step is up to him and because she has more at stake in marriage than he does, the woman will focus on his needs and self-image more than he will on hers; as a result, women who make good CP should be able to predict their boyfriends' self and ideal-self images with greater accuracy than women who do not make good CP. Conversely, the lesser importance of the woman's self and ideal-self images should be reflected in the fact that good and poor CP men should not differ as much in their ability to predict their partners' self and ideal-self concepts.

The greater importance of the man should also make his intraperceptual world more important to CP than the intraperceptual world of the woman. In other words, his perception of the satisfaction of his expectation is more important for CP than her perception in this regard. The alleged greater importance of confirming and predicting the man's self and ideal-self, and the greater importance of intraperceptual congruence for him lead to the following three hypotheses:

Hypothesis 15. *Confirmation of the man's self and ideal-self concepts through the perceptions of his girlfriend will be followed six months later by good CP, whereas confirmation of the woman's self and ideal-self concepts by the perceptions of her boyfriend will not be as strongly associated with good CP.*

In a study by the author which involved 98 unmarried couples, the following discrepancies were predicted to be significantly smaller for good CP women than for poor CP women: /self$_M$—ideal-spouse$_W$/, /self$_M$—boyfriend$_W$/, /ideal self$_M$—ideal spouse$_W$/, /ideal self$_M$—boyfriend$_W$/. All but the last discrepancy proved significant in the predicted direction. The converse measures with respect to women's self and ideal-self concepts showed only one significant result /ideal-self$_W$—ideal-spouse$_M$/, with a smaller discrepancy manifested for good CP women as opposed to poor CP women.

Hypothesis 16. *Good CP women will a) predict their boyfriends' selves and ideal-selves better than poor CP women, and b) the association between predictive accuracy and CP will be greater for women than for men.*

Both the selves and ideal-selves of good CP men were predicted significantly more accurately at the .05 and .01 points respectively by the girlfriends of good CP men as compared to the accuracy of prediction of girlfriends of poor CP men. The second half of the prediction was confirmed for the self-concept in that the biserial correlation between accuracy of prediction by women and CP was .65 while that for men was .06, the difference being significant at the .01 point. However, contrary to expectation, both men and women showed high correlations between accuracy of prediction of the ideal-self of the partner and CP. The correlation values for men and women respectively were .61 and .63, and the difference was not significant.

Hypothesis 17. *The intraperceptual congruencies (the tendency for any two perceptual sets of a person to coalesce) of good CP men should be significantly higher than for poor CP men. Since the perceptions of women have less of a determining significance, the intraperceptual congruencies of good CP women should not differ significantly from those of poor CP women.*

In the author's study of 98 couples, good CP men were significantly more congruent (less discrepant) than poor CP men on the following 8 of a total of 28 intraperceptual comparisons (all are men's perceptions) : /ideal-self—ideal-spouse/, /ideal-self—prediction of how girlfriend perceives ideal-spouse/, ideal-self—prediction of girlfriend's ideal-self/, /ideal-self—prediction of girlfriend's self/, /ideal-self—woman's prediction of boyfriend/, /perception of girlfriend—perception of how girlfriend sees boyfriend/, /self—prediction of how girlfriend sees ideal-self/, /self—prediction of how girlfriend sees self/. Only one intraperceptual comparison differentiated good and poor CP women: /boyfriend—prediction of boyfriend's perception of ideal-self/.

Hypotheses 15, 16 and 17 are, thus, generally confirmed, and the conclusion that men play a greater part in courtship than women is seemingly substantiated. Why good CP men were able to predict their girlfriend's ideal-selves better than poor CP men could, but were not

significantly better with regard to predicting their girlfriend's self-concepts is not immediately apparent and should be the object of future
research.

Two Tests of Chronological Sequence

We have essentially completed our description of the chief "stimulus,"
"value," and "role" variables. However, we have not as yet dealt with
the relationship of these variables to each other apart from noting that,
chronologically, "stimulus" variables precede "value" variables in importance, which in turn precede the effective operation of "role" variables. This, of course, is only relatively true, since information regarding
the prospective partner in all three areas becomes available from the
beginning of the relationship. However, the likelihood that certain
kinds of information will be more readily available in specific stages of
the relationship suggests that a successive filtering process occurs.
"Stimulus" variables should be most operative during the initial phases
of the relationship and least operative during the engagement period,
since by that time those couples of disparate stimulus attractiveness are
likely to have broken off their relationship. The comparison of values
through verbal interaction should not be a powerful factor in initial
"dating" since a certain amount of time is required for them to be
expressed.* Conversely, value similarity should not be strongly operative
in relationships of long duration because by that time couples with
strong value differences are likely to have separated.

Role-relationship variables should be most operative during the last
stages of the relationship prior to marriage. Because it takes a long time
to acquire information about them, they should be virtually inoperative
in the early stages of the relationship and only moderately operative
during the middle stages of the relationship. The author has collected
sufficient data to test two hypotheses regarding the effectiveness of
"stimulus" and "value" variables at different chronological periods of
the courtship process.

---

* Marriageable individuals do not, of course, usually meet on a purely random basis
with respect to values. The factors that permit them to meet often include homogamy
of wealth, educational level, and professional orientation, all of which result in their
being at a particular university. However, when I say that value similarity is not
operative in initial dating, I refer to the fact that a college group, for example, is far
less selected for "philosophical" values, which are the kinds of topics apt to be
discussed by the couples, than for the educational and social-economic values which
largely govern whether or not they meet.

Hypothesis 18. *As a "stimulus" variable, the degree of similarity of physical attractiveness between a couple should not differentiate those individuals making good CP from those making poor CP during the "role" stage of courtship.*

In the author's study of 98 couples, the discrepancy in physical attraction between good CP couples was not significantly smaller than the discrepancy between poor CP couples. The subjects had been acquainted from nine months to several years and thus could be considered to be in the "role" phase of courtship.

Hypothesis 19. *Because "value consensus" is a second-stage variable, it should not differentiate between couples making good and poor CP when progress is measured during the "role" phase of the relationship.*

In the author's study employing 99 subjects, the correlation between members of good CP couples on the author's Marriage Value Inventory was not significantly greater than that between poor CP couples during a follow-up six months after the initial testing. In a further study of 98 couples, similar negative results were obtained. Similarly, Kerckhoff and Davis (1962) reported significantly better CP for couples with high value consensus than those with lower value consensus only when couples going together less than 18 months were considered. When couples going together a longer time were examined, no significant differences were found between high and low-value consensus couples.

Last, Levinger, Senn, and Jorgensen (1970), using the Farber Index of Consensus with a sample of University of Massachusetts students, found that high-consensus couples who had a relationship greater than 18 months in duration showed significantly greater CP than did low-consensus couples. When they checked a sample of University of Colorado students, however, the low-consensus students showed the significantly greater CP in the long-term relationship. These data are confusing to say the least but suggest that much depends on the nature of the sample and the kind of instrument used. Also to be considered is how accurate the length of relationship is as a gauge of intensity of relationship. The authors of the various studies have selected 18 months as a cut-off point differentiating long and short-term relationships. Perhaps what is needed, however, is a more behavioral measure of the intensity of relationship to ascertain to what degree the couples are in the "role" stage of relationship.

In sum, it appears that there is more support for Hypothesis 19 than against it, but the mixed results clearly call for further investigation. Not only should the intensity of relationship be measured more

directly than by assuming intensity is a function of length of relationship, but more sophisticated measures of "value" are needed than
those used by Farber and Murstein.

Important Factors Not Measured

Before closing, it is necessary to describe several important factors
in marital choice which were not studied but which are important
targets for future research. The first of these is the strength of the
"desire to marry." To the extent that this variable is experienced as a
drive-state, the importance of the other factors such as assets in the
marriage market and role-compatibility should be lessened. On the
other hand, to the extent that marriage is seen as a distant or arbitrary
goal, the necessity of the existence of a near-perfect compatibility before considering marriage is increased. This variable accounts for the
fact that marriage is not entered into simply because of the compatibility between two people. Marriage, as a status, has a value in its
own right which may be considered as the summation of positive and
negative aspects as seen by the potential candidate.

The presence of the same degree of compatibility for a medical
student and his fiancée and for the skilled factory worker and his
fiancée would have rather different implications. The student would
most likely weigh the facilitative and disruptive effects of marriage
on the attainment of the M.D. degree. He also might consider
whether the choices available at the present moment might be as
wide as those available later when, as a practicing physician, his
assets in marital bargaining would be considerably elevated. This
time-perspective would probably not weigh as heavily with the factory worker who does not anticipate as great a shift in his rank in the
marital market with the passage of time. The data of Heiss (1960)
are consistent with this interpretation. He found that those groups
with the fewest occupational aspirations (women, as opposed to men;
noncollege aspirants as opposed to college aspirants) were most likely
to make good CP, but a great deal more research is needed in this area.

A factor which strongly influences the decision when to marry is that
of "expediency." An individual who is perfectly content with the status
of his relationship with his partner may be precipitated into marriage
by a change in his circumstances. A classic example of the need for
"expediency" is the unforeseen pregnancy, but a less dramatic change
of status may also affect the nature of the relationship. A man may
graduate from college and receive an offer of a job a thousand miles

away. He will need to decide whether to marry his girlfriend and take her with him or to move alone, thus curtailing and possibly severing the relationship. It is probable, therefore, that many relationships result in hasty marriages or are broken up as a function of geographical mobility.

Another factor that needs further research is the determination of how marital choice develops in a "closed field." In a "closed field" such as, for example, a classroom seminar, individuals experience a certain amount of nonstereotyped interaction regardless of whether they are drawn to each other. The effect is to weaken the influence of stimulus variables on marital choice and to maximize the influence of the second-stage or verbal-interaction variables; thus the individual who might never have been approached in an "open field" because of her limited physical attractiveness may become quite attractive to her coworker in the office as a result of luncheon conversations in the cafeteria that reveal her intelligence, sensitivity, and the similarity of her value-orientation to his own.

It is not meant to imply that, under these conditions, physical attraction completely loses its valence. Rather, the fact that the second-stage variables are given such a favorable opportunity to operate may serve to counterbalance discrepancies in physical attraction. Marriages arising as the result of "closed field" contacts may be more harmonious in later years than those arising in "open field" situations. Physical beauty wanes with age and to the extent that this variable played a part in marital selection, it might contribute to lessened satisfaction with age.

Resume of Data on Marital Choice

Nineteen hypotheses relating to SVR theory were tested and all of the hypotheses received at least moderate support. As predicted, partners possessed similar physical attractiveness and value similarity as consequences of successful passage through the "stimulus" and "value" stages of courtship. In the "role" stage, it was shown that perceived similarity or complementarity is not per se as important in understanding marital choice as is the self-acceptance of the perceiver. High self-accepting individuals were much more apt to perceive their partner as similar than low self-accepting ones. Accuracy in predicting the partner was associated with good CP, as was perceived fulfillment of ideal-spouse expectations in the partner. Because premarital couples do not have much opportunity to experience each other in a wide variety of roles, it was predicted and verified that imagined role-compatibility would greatly exceed actual role-compatibility.

Investigation of mental health showed, as predicted, that high self-accepting persons tended to pair with high self-accepting persons and neurotics with neurotics. When "normals" and neurotics paired, poorer CP was more likely to result than when members of a couple possessed similar degrees of neuroticism. Also, in accordance with exchange theory, individuals with high self-acceptance (a marital asset) were able to obtain partners closer to their expectations than were low self-accepting persons.

In the area of sex, it was predicted and confirmed that individuals with sex-drives of similar strength would tend to pair, and that the man with a high sex-drive would pose a greater threat to the viability of the relationship than the man with a low sex-drive. High-drive men, indeed, possessed less role-compatibility, were less accurate perceivers of their girlfriends, and made poorer CP than were low-drive men. There were no similar findings for women except that, as expected, good CP women showed greater sex-drive than poor CP women.

The greater importance of the man in determining CP was testified to by the fact that neuroticism in men was more inimical to CP than neuroticism in women. Further, men's greater importance as perceptual targets was evidenced by the fact that confirmation of men's self and ideal-self concepts lead to good CP, and that women's ability to predict their boyfriends' self and ideal-self concepts was also related to good CP. In addition, men's intraperceptual congruence also assured good CP. On the other hand, confirmation of the woman's self-concept, her boyfriend's ability to predict her self-concept, and her tendency towards intraperceptual congruency were not related to CP. Contrary to expectation, however, confirmation of and prediction of the woman's ideal-self concept was related to good CP.

Last, some sequence effects related to SVR theory were tested. As predicted, physical attraction, a "stimulus" variable, did not relate to CP in the "role" stage. The part played by value similarity in the "role" stage is more uncertain due perhaps to conflicting results from different studies and to the crudity of the measures of value.

The Applicability of SVR Theory to Other Dyadic Relationships

Although SVR theory was formulated to account specifically for marital choice, the behaviors and perceptions which are sufficiently rewarding to lead to marriage may also influence the formation and maintenance of other relationships. My associates and I have collected some data on two other kinds of relationships, early marriage and same-sex friendship.* These data and other published studies on marriage and friendship can test the generality of SVR theory if we, in some cases, slightly modify the hypotheses formulated earlier. Where the hypotheses have not been carried over intact, they have been changed by substituting marital adjustment (MA) in the revised hypotheses for courtship progress (CP) in the original hypotheses. For purposes of comparison, the same numeration is retained except that the letter "a" is added to distinguish the modified hypothesis from the comparable hypothesis relating to marital choice; thus, Hypothesis 3 in the former section becomes 3a when modified. Not all the hypotheses are repeated here, however, due to an absence of data bearing on the theory in these nonmarital studies.

Married Couples

Hypothesis 3, that self-acceptance is positively associated with the tendency to perceive the partner as similar to the self, has received strong support in studies by Kogan and Jackson (1964), Levy (1966), and Murstein and Beck (1971). The first study used 24 volunteer middle-aged couples who received the Interpersonal Check List. The Levy study consisted of 20 Jewish couples of an adult club of a temple who received the Gough Adjective Check List, and the last study consisted of 60 young couples who took the Norman Trait Scale (1963). In addition, Goodman (1964), using the self-reports of young married couples, reported that high self-accepting couples were *actually* more similar in their need patterns than low self-accepting couples.

Hypothesis 4a, that ability to predict the partner's self and ideal-self concepts is associated with MA, has been supported for women's predictions, but not for men's (Murstein and Beck, (1971). The findings

* The number of individuals who have worked on the marital choice, marriage, and friendship projects is, regrettably, beyond recall. I should be remiss, however, if I did not list those to whom I am especially indebted. Rosemary Burns, Richard Graf, and Neil Young served as research assistants in the "premarital" project. Gary Beck was of continuous aid in the computation and in much of the organization of all of the projects. He also did the testing for the married couples. Alexander Newman and Margaret Barnes collaborated in all phases of the "friendship" projects. Luc Jucquois and Jerry C. Lamb were of inestimable aid in the programming and computation of the endless stream of data.

are largely similar to those reported in the earlier portion of the paper on marital choice except that, in the premarital situation, men making good CP were significantly better in predicting their partners' ideal-self concepts than poor CP men. The findings in both the pre- and post-marital groups have implications for the role of men and women in marriage. Because Hypothesis 15a, below, also deals with this topic, we shall defer discussion of this topic until later.

Hypothesis 5a, that the correlation between ideal-spouse and perception of partner will be significantly associated with MA was significantly confirmed by Murstein and Beck (1971), and earlier by Luckey (1960) and Kotlar (1965). Hypothesis 6, that intraperceptions will educe significantly greater correlations than interperceptions was partially confirmed by Beck (1970). The most objective way to compare intraperceptual and interperceptual correlations is to do so for similar concepts. When, therefore, the four perceived similarity correlations (the tendency of men and of women to perceive themselves as similar to their spouses, and their ideal-selves as similar to their ideal-spouses) were averaged, they yielded a mean r of .28. Actual similarity between the couples' selves, ideal-selves, perception of partner, and ideal spouse yielded a mean r of .26, the difference between perceived and actual similarity not being significant. However, the two perceived role-compatibility correlations (perception of the spouse by one individual compared to the same person's ideal-spouse concept) averaged .48, whereas the eight actual role-compatibility correlations (self-concept of one individual compared with the way he is perceived by his spouse) showed a mean value of .30. By an exact probability test, this difference approached significance $(p < .07)$.

The eighth hypothesis, that marital partners are assortively mated for neuroticism, has found support in a number of studies. As noted in the premarital section, however, these data were obtained after marriage and assume that the neuroticism preceded the marriage. Hypothesis 9a, that MA is greater when two partners possess the same degree of mental health, has been indirectly tested by Boxer (1970). He found MA to be poor in couples where one member of the couple had been hospitalized because of a psychiatric disorder.* Compared to two control groups, the members of the psychiatric group had significantly greater discrepancies on a wide variety of measures of mental health.

---

* Boxer did not measure marital adjustment per se. However, his description of these couples plus the fact that they showed poor role compatibility (/self$_M$–spouse$_W$/; /self$_W$–spouse$_M$/) make it clear that they were dissatisfied in their marriages.

The data are not terribly strong, nonetheless, because the measurements occurred after hospitalization, and there was no way of determining the scores prior to commitment. Moreover, the couples were selected for discrepancy in that the group was defined as having *one* member who was hospitalized; accordingly, the fact that such couples diverged on mental health scores compared to control couples was not astounding. The best test of this hypothesis would obviously be a longitudinal study of intact couples.

The tenth hypothesis, that high self-accepting persons are more likely to see their spouses as approaching their ideal-spouse concept than are low self-accepting persons, was significantly demonstrated ($p < .01$) by Beck (1970) in a study of young married couples.

The greater importance of the man in courtship led to a number of hypotheses regarding his possibly greater role in determining MA. Hypothesis 14a, for example, calls for the effect of neuroticism in the man to have a greater influence on MA than neuroticism in the woman. There is very little evidence on this question. Terman (1938) found little difference between the correlation of neuroticism and MA either for men or for women. Both correlations were low and of minimal significance. His measure of neuroticism (Bernreuter's Introversion Score), however, is not considered an adequate measure by current standards. It is probably best to await further evidence before drawing any definitive conclusions with respect to this question.

Hypothesis 15a, that confirmation of the man's self-image should have greater impact on MA than confirmation of the woman's self-image, received a direct test in the Murstein and Beck (1971) article. The tendency of women to confirm the self-image of their husbands was significantly associated with MA ($p < .01$), but, as predicted, no correlation existed between MA and the confirmation of the wives' self-images by their husbands. Hypothesis 16a, that the predictive accuracy of the spouse's self and ideal-self concepts would be positively correlated with MA for female predictors but not for male predictors was also verified by this study.

The last hypothesis listed for which we have data (Hypothesis 17a), stated that if the man's role in marriage is more crucial to the success of the marriage than that of the woman, his intraperceptions should be more closely associated with the couple's MA than should his wife's intraperceptions. In the Murstein and Beck study (1971), four intraperceptions were obtained for each subject: (/self–ideal-self/; /self–spouse/; /ideal-self–ideal-spouse/; /spouse–ideal-spouse/). The average correlation for the men's perceptions was .32 and for the wives' .47.

Although the difference is not significant, a trend exists contrary to that predicted by the hypothesis and contrary to the findings in the earlier work on premarital couples.

Taken as a totality, the data in hypotheses 15a and 16a are consistent with the thesis that the husband is the central perceptual object in early marriage. Unlike the data on premarital couples, however, the present data do not support the conclusion that the husband is of major importance *both as perceiver and object.* The data from hypothesis 17a suggest that, in early marriage, either both sexes are equally important as perceivers or that the woman is somewhat more important than the man. The suggestion that the woman may be of key importance as the perceiver and the man as the perceived is quite consistent with the view, in American marriage, that the woman is called upon to adjust to the man much more than vice-versa (Burgess & Locke, 1960). If that is true, then it would be expected that her perceptions would correlate more highly with MA than his do (they do in this study, though not quite significantly). Also, correlations in which he was the perceptual target would correlate more highly with MA than when she was the perceptual target (this is largely the case). Whether this state of affairs represents an injustice to women or is an essential role differentiation necessary for optional family functioning is a point not capable of being answered by the present data.

There are, nevertheless, alternate hypotheses which could account for the data. Could it be that women are more astute about interpersonal matters than men? Perhaps so, but the data of Murstein and Beck (1971) do not reveal it. There were eight correlations in the study which measured the ability to predict the partner's responses (the self, ideal-self, spouse, ideal-spouse concepts held by the husbands and by the wives). Four of these correlations were significant at the .05 point or better; two by men, two by women. Thus, no sex difference in accuracy was observed.

When the correlations were inspected more closely, however, a pattern clearly emerged. The significant perceptions by wives were those in which they predicted their husbands self and ideal-self concepts. The significant perceptions by husbands were those in which they predicted how their wives perceived their spouses and ideal-spouses. All four significant correlations, therefore, related to the man as the perceptual object and confirm the centrality of the way the husband is perceived as a major determinant of MA.

There is, nevertheless, yet another plausible explanation of the data. It could be argued that the role of husbands in society is more clear-cut than that of women. The American male has always been called on to occupy the role of provider who aggressively surmounts any kind of difficulty while manifesting only tenderness and sensitivity towards his wife. The role of married women, however, is still in transition. Currently, we have a choice of different kinds. There is the traditional submissive wife who doesn't work but stays home and seeks to fulfill the role of good mother and homemaker. There is the career-housewife who works, tends the house, and raises the children, and feels anxious about not doing any of her jobs quite right. Then, there is the equalitarian, who insists that everything should be shared fifty-fifty.

If individuals view each other and themselves with some degree of norm stereotypy, then by following the norms in predicting the spouse's self-concept, it should be easier to predict the self-concept of the husband than of the wife. Further, to the extent that the individual conforms to the expected role for him, the couple should be happy. Since the role expected of men is so much more clearly defined than that expected of women, we would expect that satisfaction of the role norm by men should be more associated with MA than stereotyped role conformity by women.

There is a study by Corsini (1956) which bears on this question. Working with University of Chicago couples, he used a 50-item adjective Q sort to measure personality. A mean correlation resulting from every man's self sort compared with every other man's self sort served as an index of conformity to the male stereotype. A similar procedure was used to obtain a female index of conformity. The conformity index was then correlated with a measure of MA. The correlation between the MA of both husband and wife with the male conformity index was very significant; that between the female conformity index and MA, non-significant. In other words, the husband's playing a stereotyped masculine role made for a happy marriage. The wife's playing such a role was independent of MA.

With reference to the Murstein and Beck data, therefore, it may be that the accuracy in predicting the man's role is an artifact. Perhaps most of the wives predicted a socially desirable masculine role for their husbands, but only happy husbands saw themselves in this light, thus accounting for the association between accuracy and MA. The separation of these confounded explanations is a task for future research.

In sum, the research on early marriage, although skimpy, tends to support many of the hypotheses first formulated for marital choice and courtship progress. Many but not all of the factors associated with choice seem to be important in maintaining adjustment in the early years of marriage.

FRIENDSHIP

Most of the studies of friendship have utilized same-sex friends, and our conclusions are most applicable, therefore, to this kind of relationship. In the premarital data referred to earlier, the hypothesis that, in accordance with the exchange process, members of couples would show greater than chance similarity of physical attractiveness was significantly confirmed (Hypothesis 1). Few would question, however, that marriage has more of the physical in it than friendship. Also, physical appearance would appear to have greater social stimulus value in a marriage than it has in friendship; thus, we would expect either no relationship between the physical attractiveness of good friends, or at best a slight positive one.

The hypothesis was tested in a study of a girl's cooperative at Connecticut College in which everyone (N = 26) ranked every other person for physical attractiveness, the mean ranking attributed to a subject serving as the criterion. Reciprocal best friends within the group (those who chose each other among their top three friends) were correlated for physical attractiveness. The resulting r of $-.49$ ($p < .05$) was rather unexpected. It suggests that, since physical intimacy is probably not crucial to the relationship, physical attractiveness may serve as a negotiable asset on the part of an attractive woman to be traded for assets that the nonattractive friend possesses. Perhaps equal physical attractiveness on the part of girlfriends would put them in competition for the same man. It may be, therefore, that the more attractive partner serves as a model for the less attractive one on how to deal with men, which is compensated by the less attractive girl's services to the more attractive one in other areas. The data serve only to whet the appetite for more extensive research on this question.

That friends tend to share common values much more than nonfriends (Hypothesis 2) has been extensively documented by Richardson (1939, 1940), Newcomb (1961), and numerous others. The occasional failure of this variable to hold (Marsden, 1966) is a function of the nature of the control group used to compare against the friends. Marsden's data showed a significant association of values among friends, but this was no greater than the value obtained by randomly matching college girls from the same college population. If the measuring instrument deals in very general values, and if the population from which the sample is drawn is itself a homogeneous group, then it may well occur, as was the case here, that friends are no more homogeneously selected than strangers.

The tendency for self-acceptance and perceived similarity to the fiancé (e) or spouse to correlate (Hypothesis 3) was, as we have seen, well documented for engaged and married persons. The relationship also holds when best friends are substituted for the fiancé(e) and spouse (McKenna, Hofstaetter, & O'Connor, 1956; Levy, 1966; Murstein and Lamb, 1971). Hypothesis 7 called for a greater than chance correlation for self-acceptance among reciprocal best friends. In the study on the girl's cooperative (Murstein & Lamb, 1971), this was significantly demonstrated ($p < .01$). Last, several researchers (Vreeland & Corey, 1935; Bonney, 1946) have reported a correlation among friends for neuroticism (Hypothesis 8). In sum, the data on friendship closely follow the findings for premarital couples, with the noted exception of the inegality of physical attraction.

CONCLUSIONS

In reviewing the data, it appears that SVR theory is consistent with much of what we know about marital choice, and that it has applicability to other dyadic relationships such as the marital relationship and friendship. The data, in part, also resolve some of the difficulties regarding whether perceived choice is made on homogamous or complementary grounds. They show that the degree of complementarity is secondary to the pursuit of the ideal, the degree of the individual's self-acceptance, and his status in the marriage market, among other factors.

The theory is eclectic. Temporally, it is a successive filter theory; viewed at any given point of time, from a transactional point of view, it is an exchange theory; viewed teleologically, from the standpoint of the individual, it is a hedonistic theory.

Although this eclecticism aids it in accounting for much data, it also contributes to an obvious weakness. The theory bears a familial resemblance to the Austrian-Hungarian empire in that there are a considerable number of diverse elements bearing little relationship to each other and owing their presence only to the fact that they influence marital choice. This Coxey's army of recruited variables does not possess the simple elegance of the Winch or Kerckhoff-Davis theories.

In part, this inelegance must reside in my limitations as a systematist. If the theory warrants further attention, and if it generates further research, it may be that more systematic minds will amend it and give it a unity that it does not now possess.

To a certain extent, however, the heterogeneous nature of the theory is attributable to the process of marital choice itself. Perhaps no simple theory will account for marital choice because the latter is an extremely complex multidetermined act. To the layman, the complex nature of marital choice is hidden under the catch-all rubric of "love." To say that individuals marry for love, however, is to say little because "love" covers all kinds of rationales. When it accounts for everything, it accounts for nothing.

We know, from earlier research, that there are a large number of variables (age, education, propinquity, prior marital status, socio-economic status, race, etc.) which select homogamously, often before any real interaction between potential marital candidates takes place. In addition, our review has indicated that physical attractiveness, value similarity, role-compatibility, self-acceptance, sex-drive, and numerous person perception variables also influence marital choice. Although we have little data on "open" and "closed" fields, "desire to marry," and "expediency," it can scarcely be doubted that these variables are like-wise of major importance. It is doubtful that any theory can account for all of these variables on the basis of a single simple explanatory principle unless these variables are transcribed into vectors pushing the individual toward marriage or away from it. When each variable must be weighted for its positive and negative components and the correlation and interaction of the components is taken into account, however, the simple theory will probably become complex once again.

Future Direction of Research

In propounding his theory of marital choice and initiating a systematic series of quantitative studies testing the theory, Winch opened up a new era of sophistication in attacking the question of who will marry whom? From the hindsight of current thinking, and from a large number of studies, largely generated by his work, it now appears that his original theory was oversimplified, as he himself acknowledges. The work of Kerckhoff and Davis, and Berman added a degree of complexity in the theoretical thinking about marital choice. SVR theory introduces some new variables and attempts to stimulate thinking about marital choice still further.

These recent data suggest avenues which will advance our knowledge further yet. All of the theories, heretofore, have tended to view man as a sort of *tabula rasa* on whom the numerous variables act and interact. Perhaps, in all fairness, Winch should be exempted from this criticism since, in an article undertaken by his associate Ktsanes (1955), a list of various personality types emerged. Unfortunately, however, no further data along this line has emerged.

In the future, however, it may be anticipated that *differences* in marital choice will be more closely studied. The mapping of the dimensions of marital expectation (Tharp, 1963b; Ryder, 1970) will lead us in time to ask what happens when "A" is high on dimensions 1 and 2 and low on 3? What kind of person will he seek, and what is the probability of his finding and being accepted by such a person?

We shall also want to know what kind of person marries on the basis of "stimulus" variables only, and what kind takes "stimulus" and "value" compatibility into account without determining "role-compatibility?" It will also be of interest to determine each individual's *level of tolerance* of discrepancy between his expectations and his perception of their fulfillment in his partner (Hawkins, 1968).

Freed from the preoccupation of rejecting or supporting the theory of complementary needs, it would be of interest to determine under what conditions complementarity is desired and desirable. Holz's recent paper (1969) represents a start in this direction. He found that couples with traditional family ideologies tended to be complementary with respect to expressive needs and homogamous in terms of their expression of instrumental needs, whereas the situation was reversed for egalitarian dyads.

In the near future, as man solves the technological problems of his environment, the quality of his interpersonal relationships will become increasingly the center of his focus. Let us hope we shall have some answers ready for the questions he will pose.

REFERENCES

Allen G. Falling in love. *Fortnightly Review,* 1886, *46,* 432-462.
Beck, G. D. Person perception and marital adjustment. Master's Thesis, Connecticut College, 1970.
Bermann, E. A. Compatibility and stability in the dyad. Paper presented at the American Psychological Association Convention, New York City, September 1966.
Beier, E. G., Rossi, A. M. and Garfield, R. L. Similarity plus dissimilarity of personality: Basis for friendship? *Psychological Reports,* 1961, *8,* 3-8.
Berscheid, E., & Walster, E. H. *Interpersonal attraction.* Reading, Massachusetts: Addison-Wesley, 1969.
Blau, P. M. *Exchange and power in social life.* New York: John Wiley, 1964.
Boalt, G. *Family and marriage.* New York: McKay, 1965.
Bonney, M. E. A sociometric study of the relationship of some factors to mutual friendships on the elementary, secondary, and college levels. *Sociometry,* 1946, *9,* 21-47.

Bowman, C. C. Uncomplimentary remarks on complementary needs. *American Sociological Review,* 1955, *20,* 466.

Boxer, L. Mate selection and emotional disorder. *The Family Coordinator,* 1970, *19,* 173-179.

Buckingham, J. S. *The eastern and western states of America, I, II.* London: Fisher, Son & Co., 1867.

Burgess, E. W., & Locke, H. J. *The family from institution to companionship.* New York: American, 1960.

Burgess, E. W., & Wallin P. *Engagement and marriage.* Philadelphia: Lippincott, 1953.

Carter, H. & Glick, P. C. *Marriage and divorce: A social and economic study.* Cambridge: Harvard University Press, 1970.

Cattell, R. B., & Nesselroade, J. R. Likeness and completeness theories examined by sixteen personality factor measures on stably and unstably married couples. *Journal of Personality and Social Psychology,* 1967, 7, 351-361.

The choice matrimonial, *Chamber's Journal,* 1898, *1,* 498-499.

Coan, T. M. To marry or not to marry. *The Galaxy,* 1869, 7, 493-500.

Coombs, R. H. A value theory of mate-selection. *Family Life Coordinator,* 1961, *10,* 51-54.

Coombs, R. H. Value consensus and partner satisfaction among dating couples. *Journal of Marriage and the Famliy,* 1966, *28,* 165-173.

Corsini, R. J. Understanding and similarity in marriage. *Journal of Abnormal and Social Psychology,* 1956, *52,* 327-332.

Eckland, B. K. Theories of mate-selection. *Eugenics Quarterly,* 1968, *15,* 71-84.

Elder, Jr., G. H. Appearance and education in marriage mobility. *American Sociological Review,* 1969, *34,* 519-533.

English, H. B., & English, A. C. *A comprehensive dictionary of psychological and psychoanalytical terms.* New York: David McKay, 1958.

Evans, R. *Conversations with Carl Jung.* Princeton: Van Nostrand, 1964.

Fowler, L. N. *Marriage its history and ceremonies.* New York: S. R. Wells, 1855.

Fowler, O. S. *Matrimony.* Boston: O. S. Fowler, 1859.

Freud, S. On narcissim (1914). In E. Jones (ed.), *The collected papers of Sigmund Freud.* New York: Basic Books, Inc., 1959.

Sir George Campbell on scientific marriage-making. *The Spectator,* 1886, *59,* 1206-1207.

Goodman, M. Expressed self-acceptance and interspousal needs: A basis for mate selection. *Journal of Counseling Psychology,* 1964, *11,* 129-135.

Gordon, M., & Bernstein, M. C. Mate choice and domestic life in the 19th-century marriage manual. Unpublished manuscript, University of Connecticut, 1969.

Hawkins, J. L. A theory of companionate interaction. Unpublished manuscript, Indiana University, 1968.

Hegel, O. W. F. *The philosophy of right.* Chicago: Encyclopedia Britannica, 1952.

Heiss, J. S. Variations in courtship progress among high school students. *Marriage and Family Living,* 1960, *22,* 165-170.

Heiss, J. S., & Gordon, M. Need patterns and the mutual satisfaction of dating and engaged couples. *Journal of Marriage and the Family,* 1964, *26,* 337-339.

Holmes, S. J., & Hatch, C. E. Personal appearance as related to scholastic records and marriage selection in college women. *Human Biology,* 1938, *10,* 65-76.

Holz, R. F. Homogamy and heterogamy in the marital dyad: The effects of role on need dispositions. Paper presented at the American Sociological Association Convention, San Francisco, 1969.

Homans, G. C. *Social behavior: Its elementary forms.* New York: Harcourt, Brace & World, 1961.

Kerckhoff, A. C., & Davis, K. E. Value consensus and need complementarity in mate selection. *American Sociological Review,* 1962, *27,* 295-303.

Kernodle, W. Some implications of the homogamy-complementary needs theories of mate selection for sociological research. *Social Forces,* 1959, *38,* 145-152.

Kiesler, S. B., & Baral, R. L. The search for a romantic partner: The effects of self-esteem and physical attractiveness on romantic behavior. In K. Gergen and D. Marlowe (eds.), *Personality and social behavior.* Reading, Massachusetts: Addison-Wesley, 1970, pp. 155-165.

Kinsey, A. C., Pomeroy, W. B., & Martin, C. E. *Sexual behavior in the human male.* Philadelphia: Saunders, 1947.

Kinsey, A. C., Pomeroy, W. B., Martin, C. E. and Gebhard, P. H. *Sexual behavior in the human female.* Philadelphia: Saunders, 1953.

Kipnis, D. Changes in self-concepts in relation to perceptions of others. *Journal of Personality,* 1961, *29,* 449-465.

Kirkpatrick, C. A statistical investigation of the psychoanalytic theory of mate selection. *Journal of Abnormal and Social Psychology,* 1937, *32,* 427-430.

Kogan, K. L., & Jackson, J. K. Perceptions of self and spouse: Some contaminating factors. *Journal of Marriage and the Family,* 1964, *26,* 60-64.

Kotlar, S. L. Middle-class marital role perceptions and marital adjustment. *Sociology and Social Research,* 1965, *49,* 281-294.

Ktsanes, T. Mate selection on the basis of personality type: A study utilizing an empirical typology of personality. *American Sociological Review,* 1955, *20,* 547-551.

Kubie, L. S. Psychoanalysis and marriage: Practical and theoretical issues. In V. E. Eisenstein (ed.), *Neurotic interaction in marriage.* New York: Basic Books, 1956, pp. 10-43.

Levinger, G. Note on need complementarity in marriage. *Psychological Bulletin,* 1964, *61,* 153-157.

Levinger, G., Senn, D. J., and Jorgensen, B. W. Progress toward permanence in courtship: A test of the Kerckhoff-Davis hypothesis. *Sociometry,* 1970, *33,* 427-443.

Levy, M. Perceived similarity of personality as a basis for friendship and marital choice. Unpublished manuscript, Connecticut College, 1966.

Lipset, S. M., & Bendix, R. *Social mobility in industrial society.* Berkeley: University of California Press, 1959.

Luckey, E. B. Implications for marriage counseling of self perceptions and spouse perceptions. *Journal of Counseling Psychology*, 1960, 7, 3-9.

Mangus, A. H. Relationships between young women's conceptions of intimate male associates and of their ideal husbands. *Journal of Social Psychology*, 1936, 7, 403-420.

Marsden, E. Values as determinants of friendship choice. *Connecticut College Psychology Journal*, 1966, 3, 3-13.

McKenna, H. V., Hofstaetter, P. R., & O'Connor, J. P. The concepts of the ideal-self and of the friend. *Journal of Personality*, 1956, 24, 262-271.

Mittelman, B. Complementary neurotic reactions in intimate relations. *Psychoanalytic Quarterly*, 1944, 13, 479-491.

Murstein, B. I. The complementary need hypothesis in newlyweds and middle-aged married couples. *Journal of Abnormal and Social Psychology*, 1961, 63, 194-197.

Murstein, B. I. Empirical tests of role, complementary needs, and homogamy theories of marital choice. *Journal of Marriage and the Family*, 1967, 29, 689-696. (a)

Murstein, B. I. The relationship of mental health to marital choice and courtship progress. *Journal of Marriage and the Family*, 1967, 29, 447-451. (b)

Murstein, B. I. Sex-drive and courtship progress in a college sample. Unpublished paper, Connecticut College, 1970. (a)

Murstein, B. L. Love, sex and marriage throughout history. Unpublished manuscript, Connecticut College, 1970. (b)

Murstein, B. I. Self ideal-self discrepancy and the choice of marital partner. *Journal of Consulting and Clinical Psychology*, 1971, 37, 47-52.

Murstein, B. I., & Beck, G. D. Person perception, marriage adjustment, and social desirability, *Journal of Consulting and Clinical Psychology*, 1971, (in press).

Murstein, B. I., & Lamb, J. The determinants of friendship in a girl's cooperative. Unpublished paper, Connecticut College, 1971.

Newcomb, T. M. *The acquaintance process.* New York: Holt, Rinehart & Winston, 1961.

Norman, W. T. Toward an adequate taxonomy of personality attributes: Replicated factor structure in peer nomination personality ratings. *Journal of Abnormal and Social Psychology*, 1963, 66, 574-583.

Pond, D. A., Ryle, A., & Hamilton, M. Marriage and neurosis in a working-class population. *British Journal of Psychiatry*, 1963, 109, 592-598.

Rapoport, R. Normal crises, family structure and mental health. *Family Process*, 1963, 2, 68-80.

Reiss, I. L. Toward a sociology of the heterosexual love relationship. *Marriage and Family Living*, 1960, 22, 139-145.

Richardson, H. M. Studies of mental resemblance between husbands and wives and between friends. *Psychological Bulletin*, 1939, 36, 104-120.

Richardson, H. M. Community of values as a factor in friendship of college and adult women. *Journal of Social Psychology*, 1940, 11, 303-312.

Rossow, I. Issues in the concept of need complementarity. *Sociometry*, 1957, 20, 216-233.

Ryder, R. G. Dimensions of early marriage. *Family Process*, 1970, *9*, 51-68.

Schellenberg, J. S., & Bee, L. S. A re-examination of the theory of complementary needs in mate selection. *Marriage and Family Living*, 1960, *22*, 227-232.

Shuttleworth, F. K. A biosocial and developmental theory of male and female sexuality. *Marriage and Family Living*, 1959, *21*, 163-171.

Slater, E. An investigation into assortative mating. *Eugenics Review*, 1946, *38*, 27-28.

Spencer, H. *An autobiography, 1.* London: Watts & Co., 1926.

Strauss, A. The ideal and the chosen mate. *American Journal of Sociology*, 1946, *52*, 204-208.

Terman, L. M. *Psychological factors in marital happiness.* New York: McGraw-Hill, 1938.

Tharp, R. G. Psychological patterning in marriage. *Psychological Bulletin*, 1963, *60*, 99-117. (a)

Tharp, R. G. Dimensions of marriage roles. *Marriage and Family Living*, 1963, *25*, 389-404. (b)

Thibaut, J. W., & Kelley, H. H. *The social psychology of groups.* New York: John Wiley, 1959.

Thompson, W. R., & Nishimura, R. Some determinants of friendship. *Journal of Personality*, 1952, *20*, 305-314.

Turner, E. S. *A history of courting.* London: Michael Joseph, 1954.

Udry, J. R. The influence of the ideal mate image on mate selection and mate perception. *Journal of Marriage and the Family*, 1965, *27*, 477-482.

Udry, J. R., & Bauman, K. E. Skin color, status, and mate selection. Revision of paper presented at the American Sociological Association Convention, Boston, 1968.

Vreeland, F. M. & Corey, S. M. A study of college friendships. *Journal of Abnormal and Social Psychology*, 1935, *30*, 229-236.

Walster, E. The effect of self-esteem on romantic liking. *Journal of Experimental Social Psychology*, 1965, *1*, 184-197.

Walster, E., Aronson, V., Abrahams, D., & Rottman, L., Importance of physical attractiveness in dating behavior. *Journal of Personality and Social Psychology*, 1966, *4*, 508-516.

Warner, W. L., Junker, B. H. & Adams, W. A. *Color and human nature.* Washington, D. C.: American Council on Education, 1941.

Wells, S. R. *Wedlock; or the right relation of the sexes.* New York: Samuel R. Wells, 1869.

Willoughby, R. R. Neuroticism in marriage. IV homogamy: V summary and conclusions. *Journal of Social Psychology*, 1936, *7*, 19-31.

Winch, R. F. Further data and observation on the Oedipus hypothesis: The consequence of an inadequate hypothesis. *American Sociological Review*, 1951, *16*, 784-795.

Winch, R. F. *Mate-selection.* New York: Harper, 1958.

Winch, R. F. Another look at the theory of complementary needs in mate-selection. *Journal of Marriage and the Family*, 1967, *29*, 756-762.

Worthy, M., Gary, A. L., & Kahn, G. M. Self disclosure as an exchange process. *Journal of Personality and Social Psychology*, 1969, *13*, 59-63.

7

Motivation and Role:
A Comment on Balance, Reinforcement, Exchange,
Psychosomatic, and S-V-R Theories of Attraction

Robert F. Winch

The first of our papers was by Professor Theodore Newcomb and it concerned balance theory. Traditionally, balance theory has considered the relations among a person of focus (usually designated *P*), a second person (usually *O*), and a nonpersonal object (*X*). Balance implies stability; imbalance implies instability of the relationship. I gather that, to Professor Newcomb, the problem of interest is to specify conditions under which imbalance develops and exists.

According to the conventional interpretation, balance is said to exist when all signs are positive, or when two are negative and one is positive, that is, when the product of all three is positive. Imbalance is said to exist when two are positive and one is negative. Newcomb quotes Heider as saying that the situation is ambiguous when all three are negative.

In the traditional version, the location of plus and minus signs is not critical, and this is a point to which Newcomb takes exception. Since impersonal objects of attitudes do not reciprocate one's attraction, Newcomb says, a positive attitude of *P* toward *X* is not equivalent to a positive attitude of *P* towards *O*, or, in his words, humans are more sensitive to feedback from persons than from nonpersons.

152

Newcomb cites with approval the example of Abelson, who introduces the triad: Joe, Ann, and Harry. If Joe loves Ann and Ann loves Harry, then can Joe love Harry? And Newcomb believes the answer is "no" if Joe views Harry as a competitor for the affection of Ann. Momentarily, we might extend that example to the realm of animals and imagine two hungry dogs equidistant from a piece of meat which they discover at the same moment. Do we expect dog A to say, "B, old chap, I like you because of your discriminating taste in food?" Quite the contrary, in this case three pluses would make one big noisy, fur-flying minus.

It does seem that there are data such as the Joe and Harry case or the case of the two dogs in which the traditional statement of balance theory is inadequate. Thus Professor Newcomb has made a real contribution in calling this fact to our attention and asking for a modification of the theory to enable it to comprehend a broader set of data.

It seems to me that we might consider generalizing Professor Newcomb's point into a contribution to the natural history of scientific theories. It is my impression that new theories—the ones that we regard as brilliant—command our attention because they seem to explain so much with so few variables and relationships. Subsequent effort at empirical corroboration, however, typically demonstrates the reluctance of nature to parallel the parsimony of our theories. As the studies pile up, we see that more and more conditions have to be specified for the original creative insight to hold; in other words, it is necessary to add substantially to the number of variables required to establish the originally posited relationship on a completely general basis. Presently the theory becomes a special case in the corpus of the general theory of the discipline. This is, I believe, one way of interpreting Professor Newcomb's dissatisfaction with balance theory and the cases he finds that it fails to subsume.

Professor Byrne spoke to us concerning reinforcement theories and cognitive theories as complementary approaches to attraction. He emphasized that his law of attraction does not deal directly with similarity but with the effect of reinforcement on attraction. He believes that similarity (that is, the perception of similarity) is rewarding; the perception of dissimilarity is nonrewarding or perhaps punishing. I found his variation of the problem to encompass the negatively valued other to be a quite interesting one. It is, I believe, impressive that findings under somewhat varied conditions yield a linear equation with fairly steady constants. Usually we expect that mathematically expressed relationships eventually have to be curvilinear simply because otherwise our extrapolations would take us to infinity. But Byrne has overcome this problem by stating his independent variable in proportionate form and thus having the entire range from 0 to 1 under control.

I find it impressive that Byrne was able to expand his theory to take account of negatively toned similarity (and I am referring here of course to the emotionally disturbed bogus other) without having to introduce any new variable. He was able to incorporate this condition of the stigmatized other in his bivariate model.

Professor Homans is especially interested in the role of power in interpersonal attraction. He believes one would be strongly attracted to another who punishes him fairly if the punishment would enable him to learn to perform actions leading to valued rewards. In other words, Professor Homans posits a response of attraction to a stimulus of punishment and, stated in this partial and imperfect way, Professor Homans' observation is quite newsworthy. The theoretical justification of course is the eventual reward that he puts in as a necessary condition. Professor Homans' examples along this line come from the military area. I should like to offer another that comes from a somewhat different area and which illustrates, I think, in rather vivid if anecdotal form the principle that Professor Homans is enunciating. Writing at the end of the 1966 football season, Jerry Kramer (1969, p. xii), then of the Green Bay Packers, wrote that over the eight preceding seasons the Packers had been the best team in professional football, and that it was no coincidence that their coach over the exactly same period had been Vince Lombardi, whom he described as "a cruel, kind, tough, gentle, miserable, wonderful man whom I often hate and often love and always respect."

Homans sees exchange as the heart of the interpersonal relationship. He would see Lombardi and Kramer as both deriving gratification from their relationship. I am not aware, however, that he has tried to systematize the dimensions of gratification. I wish to suggest that one way—perhaps the simplest way—to differentiate categories of interpersonal relationship and gratification is to look back at the parental function. The parent of the infant nurtures—he or she gives, and the infant receives and incorporates. At a later stage—for the child's welfare as well as for the comfort of others—the parent controls the behavior of the child, i.e., is dominant whereas the child is submissive. These two dimensions of (a) nurturing and receiving and (b) controlling (or dominance-submissiveness) have been discovered in quite a variety of contexts. Before he became widely known for other activities, Timothy Leary (1957) concluded that there were two basic dimensions of his interpersonal check list. He called them love and dominance. Arthur Couch (1960, pp. 235, 554) factor-analyzed a tremendous volume of data from many of Bales's small group experiments at Harvard and found these to be his first two factors. He called them "interpersonal dominance" and "interpersonal affect." Earl Schaefer (1959) used the Guttman circumplex model on several empirical studies of maternal behavior and found two major dimensions "love vs. hostility" (our nurturance) and "autonomous control" (our dominance). And my study of complementary needs in mate selection (1958, 1967) led me to hypothesize that two basic dimensions of attraction were nurturance-receptivity and dominance-submissiveness.

I was delighted to see Professor Walster bring viscera into the dyad. Far too seldom are we reminded of man's animal nature. I do wish to comment on the nature of the conceptualization of passionate love. Since her presentation is based on the work of Schachter, I shall address my comments to his theory directly. His point is that for a full-blown experience of passion there must be both a somatic stimulus and an emotion inducing cognition. It seems implied, however, that "an emotion inducing cognition" is different from an "appropriate explanation." The former induces an emotion; the latter interprets to the *S* his somatic state *and does not induce an emotion.* Or in Schachter's words: "When either the level of sympathetic arousal is low or a completely appropriate cognition is available, the level of emotionality is low" (1964, p. 64). The common man's paraphrase might run: emotion can occur only when a man doesn't know why he feels funny.

Now I have trouble translating that conclusion into the context of love. The implication seems to be that passionate love is possible only if we asume that the lover experiences sympathetic arousal and attributes it to a false cause; in other words, if the *E* should explain to the *S* that the *S*'s erection resulted from foreplay with a desirable and attractive woman, the explanation should suffice to calm the *S*.

One other observation I have concerning this formulation has to do with an absence of a longer-range interactional context. The presentation makes the theory seemingly applicable to short episodes having no history and no sequel. What would be the outcome if we assume that the individuals involved had known each other for some time as, for example, in the case of a middle-aged married couple?

I turn now to Professor Murstein's paper. Since it concerns marital selection, it is appropriate to comment on the societal context within which it may be presumed to operate. It is evident that Murstein has in mind a form of mate selection wherein the principals to a marriage select each other and have some available options as to such selection. Thus the society is one in which the field of eligible spouse-candidates is fairly wide. Moreover, it follows that both the extended family and the nuclear family are relatively functionless. The extended family is virtually functionless because of the fact that the principals are free to choose each other. Where the extended family is more functional, it is frequently the case that marital selection is far too important a matter to the family to be left to inexperienced, naive young people. Moreover, the nuclear family is toward the less functional end of the spectrum because of the fact that Murstein implies selection will be for expressive rather than instrumental roles, i.e., for love rather than for money or muscle.

It is under these conditions, Murstein implies, that a stimulus-value-role theory of marital choice is presumed to operate. Parenthetically, I might add that it is also under these conditions that I have hypothesized that the theory of complementary needs would work. Professor Murstein speaks of his theory as filtering and hedonic and involving the idea of exchange. These remarks apply as well to the theory of complementary needs, although I should like to qualify the remark about exchange in the sense that I have already noted in my discussion of Professor Homans' paper—namely, that the variables of interpersonal attraction and gratification should be specified.

Professor Murstein says that his theory is sequential. It follows that during the stimulus stage couples are presumed to be sorted out so that they are roughly similar to each other. That is, they are expected to show intra-pair homogeneity with respect to physical attractiveness and, in the second stage, with respect to values. I have argued that such similarity can be expected as a consequence of differential association and the field of eligibles.

Of the 19 hypotheses Murstein tests in his paper, one is devoted to the stimulus stage and one to the value stage. Of the remaining 17, 11 are allocated specifically to the role stage—four subsumed under the rubric "perceived role fit," four under "personal adequacy," and three under "sexual compatibility." In addition, four hypotheses are presented under the heading "the greater importance of the man in courtship," and two under "tests of chronological sequence." I gather that the first four of these six should be interpreted as pertaining to sex roles, and therefore that Murstein has allocated a total of 15 out of the 19 hypotheses to the role stage of his theory. Presumably this implies that he regards the third stage as the scientifically most important part, a judgment with which I should agree.

It is the role stage of Murstein's theory, however, that I find most difficult to work with. I have no trouble agreeing with him that the notion of role pertains to expectations about behavior appropriate to a position in a social system. Missing from his formulation, however, is an element I regard as important. This element is the stipulation that role involves the idea of consensus about those expectations. For example, our culture reflects a great deal of agreement on how a bank teller is to treat a depositor, and how a shoe salesman is to treat a customer. Perhaps I should emphasize that when I use the term "consensus" I am referring to a state of affairs in which there is society-wide agreement that serves to define a role, or at least where there is substantial agreement in some meaningful subsocietal category, e.g., white middle-class college students at Ivy-League colleges or young urban black militants. Murstein does not specify the elements of the consensual description of the role or roles he is considering.

Perhaps the reason Murstein has not described the roles of interest here is that he believes there is not much consensus as to their characteristics for our culture to reflect. Does our culture portray the traits of a good husband and of a good wife? If Murstein believes that the culture is not very definite on this point, I am prepared to agree with him and to remark that this is a consequence of a relatively functionless state of the nuclear family. But I should argue that it is precisely this state of affairs that renders the utility of the concept of role very questionable in this context. Starting from what I construe to be a quite similar point of view in this matter, I did not try to make use of the notion of role in my study of complementary needs.

What Murstein has actually done in this section of his paper is to work with the ideas of similarity and dissimilarity of ego and alter, of ideal ego and ideal alter. It need hardly be noted that such similarity—ipsative or dyadic at most—is not what I have referred to above as consensus. Moreover, Murstein has revealed little of the nature of the variables entering into that ipsative or dyadic similarity. What dimensions are involved? Can any inferences be drawn from these dimensions as to the nature of consensually defined dating or spousal roles? The lack of specification with respect to the relevant dimensions of similarity and the consequent lack of any content of the concept of role constitute the nub of the difficulty I experience with Murstein's use of the concept of role. Here is a point Murstein's stimulus-value-role theory shares with balance theory, with reinforcement theory of attraction, and with exchange theory. None of these papers specifies the trait content or role content of liking or of similarity.*

---

* Perhaps it is useful (a) to point out that this lack of specification of the content of similarity is part of the difficulty Murstein refers to in Chapter 1 where he mentions the variety of idiosyncratic reward systems and the resulting hazard of using reward in a circular logic, and (b) to suggest that to specify such dimensions in advance of data-gathering avoids this hazard. My effort along this line appears in Winch, 1958, Table 1, page 90.

In this connection it is useful to recall the study done some years ago by Eric Bermann. His subjects were student nurses. He was trying to predict the stability of dyads of roommates on the basis of complementary needs and of compatibility of roles. He found that he could predict on the basis of complementary needs, could predict somewhat better on the basis of role theory (oriented to the subjects' role as student nurse), and considerably better still on the basis of the two theories combined.

Murstein has not specified the social system whose positions are of research interest in his theory of marital choice. It seems likely that he intends us to understand that the social system of interest is the marital dyad. It is at this point that Bermann's design is suggestive, for it points out that the system of reference may be something other than the dyad itself. For example, let us think of a married couple who happen to be graduate students of, say, sociology. Let us assume also that they met while they were both graduate students. In the process of becoming attracted to each other it seems quite obvious that they would have assessed each other on the basis of (a) competence of reading and understanding the professional literature, (b) competence of oral presentation of such materials, (c) creativity in ideas, (d) competence in creativity in methodology, (e) esteem of other graduate students, (f) esteem of various members of faculty, etc. Each of the lettered items in the preceding sentence might be regarded as one of the constituent roles making up the position of graduate student in the social system consisting of faculty, graduate students, and more or less peripheral personnel.

This maintains the situation set forth in Bermann's presentation, i.e., the two parties are members of a common social system larger than the dyad. Another arrangement of course would be one wherein each assesses the other as a member of a system in which the assessor does not participate. If the man were a sociologist and the woman an economist, such would be the case.

What follows from the foregoing remarks? First, I think it is clear that if we are to use the concept of role in establishing the theory of attraction in mate selection, it is important for us to specify the social system or systems of reference. Second, it is relevant to note whether or not the two individuals are in a situation of actual or potential competition. Third, insofar as the men and women under consideration are involved in occupations, there can always be some implicit element of competition even though they are not participating in a common social system. Here I refer to the fact that the explicit and manifest reward of occupational performance is money, and the fact that each is rewarded in this common medium makes it possible to assess on one nation-wide standard the esteem in which each is held.

Now I should like to offer some overall and, hopefully, integrating remarks. We seem agreed that, ceteris paribus:

1. X will find Y attractive if Y rewards X.
2. The more Y rewards X the more X will find Y attractive.
3. There are two kinds of reward:
   a. being liked and approved
   b. perceiving the other as similar to the self. (Byrne, 1969, says we like people who agree with us because of consensual validation, i.e., they offer evidence our position is correct.) Both the data of Byrne and of Murstein indicate that this should be qualified in that similarity to a negatively regarded other is not rewarding.
4. We are also reminded that reward may be conceptualized both cognitively and somatically.

I believe it is time to try to foresee possible promising next steps.

First, I believe we should operationalize our dependent variable—attraction—so that we can speak confidently about the explained variance. For example, Newcomb asks under what conditions are forces toward interpersonal balance outweighed by other forces? But we don't know—do we?—what proportion of the variance in some specified population is "explained" by balance theory or is left "unexplained."

Second, as I understand it, toward the close of his paper Professor Newcomb has endorsed taking role theory into account. In my comments on Professor Murstein's paper I expressed my views on this idea. Newcomb has also proposed taking a longitudinal view so as to take account of changes in interpersonal attraction. This seems to me a sterling idea.

Third, I think it is desirable to regard the nature of the reward as highly problematic. What other rewards result in attraction besides the perception of the other as similar to the self and that the other likes and approves the self?

H. A. Murray (1968) has discussed what he calls hedonic and anhedonic determinants (or generators) for behavior. Classifying such determinants by location, he says they may be located within the actor or in the environment. This is especially true of interpersonal transactions.

With respect to the first set (somatic determinants) Murray suggests that some are emotional (e.g., love, hate, fear) and are located in the center of the subcortex; some are sensory, imaginal, conceptual, verbal, or motor (and he speaks of these as processional determinants) ; and some are judgments of conscience (or superregnant determinants). It seems to me that if such a classification of hedonic determinants is useful it may be in order to conceptualize rewards similarly.

Murray goes on to remark that in the early months of life environmental generators are dominant in the sense that they control one's pleasure and pain, one's comfort and discomfort. Later, however, several other kinds of determinants are more important: such central determinants as fantasies and dreams, such achievement determinants as the ambition to control one's own processes and to compete successfully, and such transactional determinants as those that result in the emission from others of acceptance, inclusion, promotion, respect, affection, lust-love, and their opposites. Moreover, he reminds us, as have Schachtel, Maslow, and Robert White, that man is not a creature of habit alone but also that he possesses a self-realizing, novelty-seeking, creative disposition. And of course I do not need to remind you that this observation directs our attention away from tension-reduction and toward tension-seeking.

Fourth, Aronson (1970) has data on some points of interest:

1. Although we are attracted to competent others, our attraction is heightened by evidence that the competent person is fallible. Aronson's study was stimulated by the fact that President Kennedy's popularity rose after the Bay of Pigs fiasco. He called his study "The effect of a pratfall on increasing inter-personal attractiveness."
2. Lamenting that physical attractiveness was rarely investigated as an antecedent of liking, Aronson showed that beauty produced some interesting interactional effects.
3. Proceeding from what he calls his gain-loss theory, he has shown that we are more attracted to people whose esteem of us is increasing than we are to people who have continuously held us in high esteem. He also speaks of this as his "law of marital infidelity."

It might be useful to conceive of this finding as subsumable under the general heading of adaptation, or perhaps of relative gratification and relative deprivation. We may recall findings from studies of sensory deprivation to the effect that, as the input of stimuli decreases, sensitivity increases so that the subject attains his maximum sensitivity under conditions of minimum stimulation.

We may recall also that the studies of the American soldier in World War II (Stouffer et al, 1949, pp. 250-258) revealed that when rank, educational level, and length of service were held constant, the *less* the opportunity for promotion, the *more* favorably did the soldiers assess their chances for promotion. The explanation, which gave rise to the term "relative deprivation," was that the individual was evaluating his chances of promotion in comparison with the chances of others who shared his situation.

This same principle may be invoked in another study Aronson cites that led to the conclusion that "people like similar people better than people they convert to their way of thinking" unless they are ego-involved with converting them . . . in which case they like the convert better" (Aronson, 1970, p. 164). This calls to mind Shaw's *Major Barbara* in which one client at the Salvation Army urges another to present himself as an extensive sinner, for then the members of the Salvation Army would feel so good about saving his soul.

In conclusion, it seems to me that we may push ahead in the following ways:

1. We might explore the kinds of outcomes in dyadic interaction that lead to positive and negative cathexes and hence are positive and negative rewards. By this I mean we ought to look at the broad spectrum of hedonic generators of which Murray speaks.
2. We might pay heed to the level of adaptation of the subjects. That is, we should note the level and sources of gratification and frustration and deprivation that the subject is experiencing aside from his interaction with the particular other.
3. Level of expectation is also of conceivable relevance. What does the subject think he should get from the relationship? What does he think others in parallel situations are getting?
4. If role theory is to be used, I believe it is necessary to specify the social systems under consideration as well as the specific positions and roles involved in the analysis.

REFERENCES

Aronson, E. Some antecedents of interpersonal attraction. In William J. Arnold & David Levine (eds.), *Nebraska Symposium on Motivation,* 1969. Lincoln, Nebraska: University of Nebraska Press, 1970, pp. 143-177.

Bermann, E. Compatibility and stability in the dyad. Paper presented before the American Psychological Association, New York, September 1966.

Couch, A. S. Psychological determinants of interpersonal behavior. Unpublished doctoral dissertation, Harvard University. 1960.

Kramer, J. *Instant replay.* New York: Signet, 1969.

Leary, T. *Interpersonal diagnosis of personality: A functional theory and methodology for personality evaluation.* New York: Ronald, 1957.

Murray, H. A. Components of an evolving personological system. In David Sills (ed.), *International encyclopedia of the social sciences.* New York: Macmillan, 1968, *12*, 5-13.

Schachter, S. The interaction of cognitive and physiological determinants of emotional state. In Leonard Berkowitz (ed.), *Advances in experimental social psychology, 1.* New York: Academic Press, 1964, pp. 49-80.

Schaefer, E. S. A circumplex model for maternal behavior. *Journal of Abnormal and Social Psychology,* 1959, *59*, 226-235.

Stouffer, S. A., Suchman, E. A. et al. *The American soldier, 1.* Princeton, N. J.: Princeton University Press, 1949.

Winch, R. F. *Mate-selection: A study of complementary needs.* New York: Harper and Row, 1958.

Winch, R. F. Another look at the theory of complementary needs in mate-selection. *Journal of Marriage and the Family.* 1967, *29*, 756-762.

Index

Index

Author Index

A

Abelson, R. P., 37, 42, 79, 81
Abrahamsson, B., 19, 20
Adams, W. A., 17, 115
Allen, G., 102
Anderson, N. H., 70
Aponte, J. F., 63
Aristotle, 23, 53
Aronson, E., 10, 11, 12, 27, 61, 66,
    94, 160, 161

B

Backman, C. W., 7
Baldridge, B., 63
Bales, 154-155
Baral, R. L., 113, 128
Baskett, G. D., 7
Bauman, K. E., 17, 115
Beck, G. D., 139, 140, 141, 142, 143
Bee, L. S., 107
Beier, E. G., 8
Bendix, R., 115
Bermann, E. A., 107, 146, 158
Bernreuter, 141
Bernstein, M. C., 101
Berscheid, E., 41, 85, 116
Blau, P., 18, 19, 47, 48, 49, 113

Boalt, G., 108
Bond, M. H., 6
Bonney, M. E., 145
Boulding, K. E., 19
Bowman, C. C., 107
Boxer, L., 140
Brehm, J. W., 92
Brewer, M. B., 70
Brewer, R. E., 70
Buckingham, J. S., 100
Burgess, E. W., 108, 129, 142
Burnstein, E., 35
Byrne, D., 2, 3, 5, 6, 7, 9, 10, 12,
    13, 14, 15, 59-81, 63, 64, 65,
    67, 68, 70, 71, 75, 76, 77,
    153-154

C

Campbell, D. T., 7
Carter, H., 17, 115
Cartwright, D., 23, 79
Cattell, R. B., 108
Chase, C. A., 17
Christie, R., 43
Clore, G. L., 5, 63, 64, 65, 70
Coan, T. M., 102
Collins, B. E., 22, 24
Commins, W. D., 7

DATE DUE